ONLINE Teaching SIMPLIFIED

Powerful and Practical Tools and Tips to Help Teachers Maximise the Online Teaching-Learning Process

RANDY BENTINCK

B.A. Degree Fine Arts (Hons), **Dip Ed.** (Admin)

FYAPUBLISHING | GEORGETOWN

Randy Bentinck/FyaPublishing

95 South Turkeyen,

Georgetown, Guyana.

Online Teaching Simplified/ Randy Bentinck

ISBN 9798215841426

Dedicated to the teachers and educators who are teachable and recognize that change is an integral part of growth

"If we teach today as we taught yesterday, we rob our children of tomorrow."

— John Dewey

TABLE OF CONTENTS

INTRODUCTION:

The Benefits of Teaching Online

"Education is the most powerful weapon that we can use to change the world."
– Nelson Mandela

Will technology replace teachers?

Technology will never replace teachers, but teachers who are not technologically competent will be replaced by teachers who are.

If you are in the business of education and you are not technologically competent and the answer to the question doesn't move you to stop and think seriously, then you will soon be replaced!

Education is a business and whether you are teaching or lecturing in a private or public institution, you must adapt and change to suit the changing technology landscape in education or perish.

You are about to learn information that will help you simplify the online teaching-learning process and have you crushing it like a boss!

What is the value of online education?

The internet has changed the way we communicate with one another as well as how we access, share, and facilitate information sharing. The challenge is no more how to use technology to teach, but how teachers grasp how the world is changing. Teachers must understand the value of online literacy and the role collaboration and online engagement play in teaching and learning.

Software and technology are growing at dizzying speed, and it's difficult to keep up. As a result, rather than focusing on the technology itself, effective pedagogical techniques for online teaching must be identified.

Teachers who Teach Online have the Advantage of:

Increased time flexibility:

Teachers who teach online enjoy increased flexibility in the way they use their time with students. Learning can take place at more convenient and effective periods for both students and teachers. Students can work at their own pace within a set framework, and the online learning and teaching engagement process can be divided into smaller, more regular chunks of time.

Locational flexibility has increased:
For teachers who teach online, the teaching and learning can take place anywhere (home, office, while commuting, or even in coffee shops) and can include students and teachers from all over the world.

Context:
Teachers who teach online provide their students with online education that exposes them to a wider variety of new and relevant information in today's ever-changing technology landscapes. It prepares students to make a smooth transition to higher education and in professional and industry activity.

Information exchange:
Teachers who teach online have the advantage of easy access to a wider variety of educational resources. This makes it easier and more convenient to access and share relevant information with their students at the click of a mouse. Teachers and students can join online communities or practice depending on their interests rather than their geographical location.

Internet resources:
Teachers who teach online expose their students to a broader range of internet resources and knowledge.

An extensive and enlightening experience:
Teachers who teach online can create conditions that can improve student learning by allowing for cross-disciplinary, cross-cultural, and/or cross-campus partnerships. This learning experience can take place on a local, national, or international scale, and it can be enhanced by improved contact and participation, peer feedback, and group work skills.

Disability, equity, and access:
Teachers who teach online provide a means for equal opportunity for students who have a handicap or who have accessibility issues that make it difficult for them to attend a face-to-face lesson.

Information literacy in the digital age:
Teachers who teach online helps to foster digital literacy skills in their students, which is of vital importance in today's tech-dominated culture and business environment.

Now that we have been exposed to the invaluable benefits of teaching online, let us examine how to go about planning your lesson to maximise your online teaching experience.

CHAPTER ONE:

Planning an Effective Online Lesson

"Nothing is so fatal for a teacher as unpreparedness" - Davis

The extent to which you know your learners or audience will go a long way toward assisting you in creating compelling instructional material.

While there are numerous methods for creating and delivering content online, it is critical to have a clear plan describing how you should go about it and selecting the appropriate manner to incorporate it.

Key Components of a Digital Lesson Plan

Creating and executing your online lessons will go much smoother if you are prepared.

It will not be a pleasant experience for you nor your students if you wing it for 25 or 40 minutes in front of the camera, so make sure your lesson plan includes the following components:

An Objective or a Statement of Learning Objectives

Your digital lesson plan is built on objectives. They should be stated clearly and define which skills, knowledge, or understanding students are anticipated to achieve as a result of the lesson. For example, "At the end of this lesson, students will be able to observe and recognize all countries that make up the United Nations."

Make sure your goals are practical, measurable, and in line with your school's and/or district's educational standards for your grade level.

Materials Needed

Make a list of all the resources that will be needed and make sure they are available well in advance of the session. Digital textbooks, PDFs, and other online learning resources are examples of this. Make sure you have digital versions of content on hand to give to your students.

Include any links or material that you believe will be useful in your lesson. Make sure your sites are bookmarked and playlists are ready ahead of time.

Instructions and Procedure

Make precise notes on both the digital lesson or activity process and how instructions are to be presented. Maybe there's certain knowledge you don't want students to know right away, but you want them to find it as the session progresses.

Your online lesson plan template should be detailed enough so that everybody who reads it has the same information and ability to teach the lesson properly.

Lesson and Activity Group Sizes

Individuals, pairs, small groups, and whole-class work are all appropriate groupings for activities in your classes. For online lessons, you can use chat and video services to help with this.

Consider which groupings will work best for each activity when designing your activities, or whether students will have the choice of picking which group sizes work best for them.

A Technique for Measuring Student Progress Towards Goals

How will you know whether your digital lesson plan was successful in meeting the learning objectives? Detail your formative assessment procedure (oral quiz, written quiz, project, etc.) in your online lesson plan, and get comments on what worked and didn't work for students.

Determine which values will be utilized to define the success of your lesson (example: students can display knowledge comprehension in line with the learning objective 80 percent of the time).

Follow up on your lesson with any appropriate homework tasks to extend learning. Completing homework can assist your students in broadening their knowledge.

Preparing Lesson Plans Online

Aim to have digital lesson plans finished a day or two before they are to be implemented. This will allow time to assess and change objectives if needed.

For generating lesson plans, several schools and districts demand the usage of lesson planning books and templates. If yours does not, or you are teaching in another country with different policies, you can make your own online lesson plan template or get one from the internet. With little instruction and practice, you'll be well on your way to learning how to create your lesson plan.

Effective Classroom Management Requires Digital Lesson Planning

Digital lesson planning is critical to providing students with a solid online classroom environment that promotes their learning. Students of all ages respond best to predictable routines in which they are involved and aware of the process and can expect what will happen next.

During difficult circumstances, children look to their academic routine to keep them on track. Post your lesson plans in many public areas online so that students, substitutes, and parents can all see them and keep on track with your curriculum.

A digital lesson plan for teachers that considers students' learning styles and interests can increase student engagement and involvement. Encourage your students to provide feedback on lessons during the week or at the end of a completed lesson and keep track of which parts elicited the greatest and worst replies.

Creating a strong digital lesson plan format,

like any skill, becomes easier with practice. It may appear to be a daunting task at first, but if you are consistent, you will eventually discover your rhythm.

The most crucial aspect of the process is to always consider the requirements of your students, including yourself as a teacher.

Creativity in class planning is crucial, but keep your budget and time constraints in mind, and don't overextend yourself.

Important lesson plan components

You should aim to include each of these procedures in each lesson you teach:

1. Engage

The initial step in your online teaching lesson should be to engage the student by activating prior learning. Get their minds thinking in terms of your specific subject area and make them apply what they already know right away.

Engagement activities are excellent warm-ups. Depending on the student's level, and your subject area, you can play a game, teach a song, or have them repeat a chant.

2. Explain

You will introduce fresh material and ideas

to your students during the explanation stage of your lesson. If you're teaching a language class, for example, you can use vocabulary words, say them out loud first and then have your students repeat them. You can also teach the meaning of certain words to more advanced students.

Introduce grammatical subjects like verb tenses to the student here if you're teaching them. This is also an excellent opportunity to pre-teach any tough vocabulary or topics in a reading piece.

3. Elaborate

Allow your students to investigate the material under your supervision. This might be a topic-related reading passage or blog, a matching game, or a movie/video that the student sees and discusses.

You should encourage your students to communicate independently throughout this time, although you can help if they are having difficulty.

4. Evaluate

Allow the students to demonstrate what they've learnt at the end of the class. This is an unguided activity in which the student demonstrates their ability to utilise the material they have acquired independently.

Just remember that if you plan to use a song or video, download it before the lesson time and make sure you can pull it up quickly.

Effective Lesson Design

A well-designed online teaching session aids in student learning, retention, and engagement.

Whether you are generating learning material for your remote learning students or constructing an online course for a potential target audience, the online lesson planning strategies described below will assist you in doing so successfully. You will be able to generate something that satisfies the needs of all students.

Recognize Your Students

The audience distinguishes an online course from an online classroom. Your virtual classroom audience consists of students you know well and who are generally of the same age and circumstances as you. Because you are already aware of their learning patterns, skills, and shortcomings, creating a lesson plan to meet their needs is much easier.

If you are not, you might begin by assessing their previous knowledge using a quiz or a simple brief activity such as a concept map. Those who take an online course, on the other hand, may come from anywhere in the world, speak different languages, and have various reasons for learning the subject you are giving. As a result, taking the extra time to properly investigate who your students are will assist you in designing a lesson that will provide significant value to them.

Set a Specific Goal for the Lesson

A clear purpose is vital for staying focused throughout your lesson's course plan, and it should be highlighted to your students from the start to assist them to stay on track.

The goal of your class should be to focus on what your students will be able to accomplish at the end of it. For example, it may be to assist your students in learning a new skill or understanding a new concept. To establish a clear goal, begin with "I want my students to be able to..."

This simplifies the process of defining the material because what should be included in your session is what will ultimately help your student reach the set target.

Include visuals, visuals, and even more visuals.

Keeping students' attention while teaching a class face-to-face is tough enough. How do you make an impression when you aren't even present?

According to educational experts, individuals recall 80% of what they see, 20% of what they read, and 10% of what they hear, which is why images play a crucial part in teaching, especially when it is done online.

Here are a few examples of how you can use graphics in your lessons:

Video instructions are being used in place of textual instructions. Instead of sending them a document that explains something, make a fast video that explains it.

Captions and transcriptions (which students with hearing problems will appreciate) can be added to your videos to provide assistance and underline crucial points your audience should remember.

If recording a video is too time-consuming or technical for you, or if you are in a hurry, you may find a relevant video that already exists on the internet.

Here are some significant sources to use:

- <u>YouTube Learning</u>

- <u>BBC Bitesize</u>

- <u>Google Videos</u>

- <u>National Geographic Education</u>

- <u>History</u>

Graphic organizers are another excellent technique to clarify a complex idea while also capturing your students' attention during your class or lecture session. The Ultimate Collection of Graphic Organizers for Teachers and Students is a comprehensive list of graphic organizers for reading, writing, comparing, and other activities.

- Make use of an online whiteboard. When an idea is too complex for words, you can always use your whiteboard/blackboard to sketch down or illustrate it in class. You can do the same thing using an online whiteboard. *Creately* is extensively used in online classes by educators for this purpose; its endless online canvas, access to shape libraries for over 50+ diagram kinds, and pre-made templates allow them to readily visualize what they need for their lecture. Furthermore, thanks to its in-app video conferencing, you can host the lesson in Creately while working with students on the same canvas with synchronous editing.

•   Presentations are excellent visual tools for engaging students both in class and online. While a presentation can be used to describe a complete subject, it may also be used to highlight essential facts during an online class session. You can also use a tool like *Prezi* to make narrated presentations.

•   During an online class, employ visual aids. Props might range from flashcards to everyday items found in your home. For example, if you're talking about different sorts of nourishing food, you're bound to have a few props lying about your house.

Maintain Your Teaching Modules Timing is critical in online learning.

•   A long online lecture can quickly disengage students and make it difficult for them to digest the material. As a result, it is critical to keep things brief and entertaining.

•	As previously suggested, incorporate a range of visual components within your lessons/course. Visuals will help to simplify tough topics that might otherwise necessitate lengthy discussions.

•	Divide the lesson content into sections. You can, for example, develop a short video instructional series or a blog post series to deliver the lesson in discrete pieces that students may view or read at their leisure.

•	Turn your classroom upside down. The flipped classroom method has been shown to boost student engagement and retention, particularly in online learning. Allow students to complete in-class tasks (such as watching video lectures, reading documents, or listening to a podcast) before the real class while supporting and guiding them as they complete homework during the class. This way, you can leave the dull lecture portion of the session for students to complete at their own pace and make better use of in-class time.

Maintain a Consistent and Clear Structure

To keep learners involved and focused, a constant and clear structure is essential. Creating an overview covering all modules, tasks, tools, due dates, and so on at the start is an easier method to maintain a clear and consistent framework throughout your lesson or course planning. Create a solid lesson plan, in other words. This will assist you in identifying theme subjects and organizing them as modules or units with a decent flow.

You can also assist your students by:

- Keeping all instructional materials, assignments, and other resources in a central location that is easily accessible to all students. You can do this by using a file storage system like *Google Drive* or your school's learning management system.

- Make a list of what topics such as, chapters, modules, units. that will be covered each day or week. Along with the checklist, you may include the assignments they will be working on as well as the resources and equipment they will need. You can make this along with your lesson plan and distribute it to your students to help them stay on track with their work.

Include Assignments and Homework. Assignments are an important aspect of learning and an efficient way to assess students based on what they have learned.

This is possible in online learning by:

- Activities that require collaboration are included. Having students work in groups and communicate with one another while they attempt to comprehend something can improve their understanding and recollection.

- Provide the essential platforms to help with this, such as a communication tool like **Slack**, **WhatsApp Group** or a **Facebook Group** for students to communicate and share resources, or an online discussion board.

- If you are concerned about cheating during online assignments, you can add tasks that require students to conduct research and create, such as case studies, concept maps, videos or presentations, speeches, and so on.

Examine, Reflect, and Revise

How do you know what works and what doesn't when it comes to online lesson planning? Evaluating and modifying the tactics, content, and technologies you use to deliver a lesson online is critical to improving your students' learning environment, whether online or in-person.

The more you assess and evaluate, the better your chances of developing learning material or an entire course that resonates with your students.

To properly measure the success of your course or lesson content, you can utilize an instructional design methodology such as the *ADDIE* (analyze, design, develop, implement, and evaluate) model.

You can also encourage students to provide comments to gain an understanding of what was effective from their point of view.

A well-prepared lesson plan without the suitable hardware to execute online will ruin the online teaching experience for you. The next chapter will provide some examples of hardware that you may use to make things simpler for you.

CHAPTER TWO:

The Best Hardware for Online Teaching

"Technology is just a tool. In terms of getting the kids working together and motivating them, the teacher is most important."
– Bill Gates

This hardware list is a guide to assist you in taking your online teaching game to the next level. Most of the recommendations are within a realistic price range. For example, for about $100, you can add a whole green screen system, including the backdrop, stands, and even the lights. Included as well are several low-budget solutions because you don't need the best equipment to convey your ideas and lessons.

Please note that prices change over time, so by the time you read this book, prices may have changed or a better product will be available.

Learning retention, whether online or not, is determined by the quality of the lesson and the tools available to facilitate the teaching-learning process.

Let that be a source of optimism for all teachers who are suddenly thrust into the world of online learning. Sure, having amazing equipment is important (and never underestimate the value of pleasant sound), but you don't need a high-tech studio to spread knowledge across the internet.

Before we continue, one more word of caution: Online teaching jumped from a niche practice to a must-have with the onset of COVID-19. Gear is in extraordinary demand, and that means a lot of big brand items are out of stock. It also implies that unethical individuals are price gouging and scalping.

Don't overpay for your equipment. Either wait or look for a less expensive alternative.

In some instances, you can even buy used ones. Don't give in to the criminals who want to profit on your quest to continue learning, even if you're at home and amid a pandemic. Now let's look at the recommended list...

Blue Yeti USB Microphone

Your primary concern should be how you sound.

You might think that teaching over video necessitates excellent video quality, but it is sound quality that is most important. You may get away with lesser frame rates and even pixilated video, but if your sound is irritating, your students will quickly tune you out.

The Blue Yeti produces consistent high-quality sound. It comes with a variety of pickup patterns, giving you some flexibility in how you use it.

Buying Tip: because of the epidemic, these are in and out of stock. If one colour is out of stock, try another colour. Also, don't be fooled by price gougers: this should cost around $130 new.

<u>Budget Option:</u> For about $10, you can get away with something simple, like this budget headset. It provides an acceptable microphone (who are we kidding?) a headset speaker, and because it is over-the-head, there is no need for a stand.

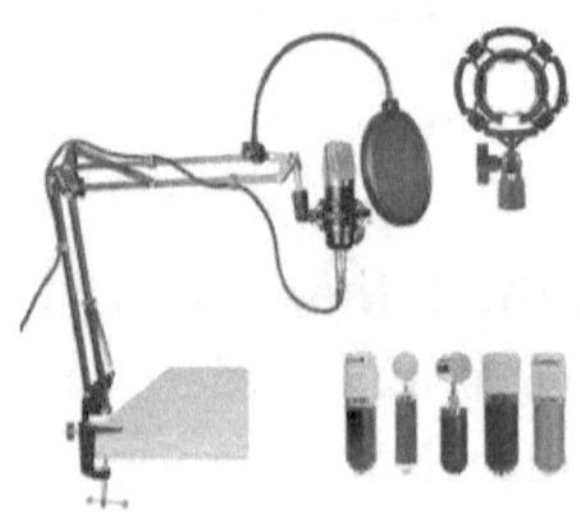

RODE PSA 1 Microphone Boom Arm

RODE PSA 1 is a strong boom arm with a fair reach.

As a teacher/tutor, you will spend a lot of time in front of a microphone when teaching online, and you want it to come to you rather than you having to stoop down to reach it. Your back will appreciate it.

Using the RODE microphone arm will go a

long way in making your teaching experience more comfortable.

Microphone Pop Filter

Peter Piper, who chose a pound of pickled peppers.

The puff of air that comes out of your mouth when you start a word with "p." Microphones pick up on that rise in air pressure and magnify it to where it's quite irritating to listen to. This too can take away from the online teaching experience for your students.

The solution is simple. Insert a pop filter. There is no magic to employ. You will find this type to be very useful. It's a small additional cost given the advantage it delivers and if you are so inclined, you can make a DIY alternative. There are lots of videos on YouTube that will show you step-by-step.

Sennheiser Headphones

Sennheiser is a manufacturer of audio equipment.

They're great, high-quality headphones that aren't too expensive. They're also unobtrusive if you need to use them on camera because they're black with no sparkle.

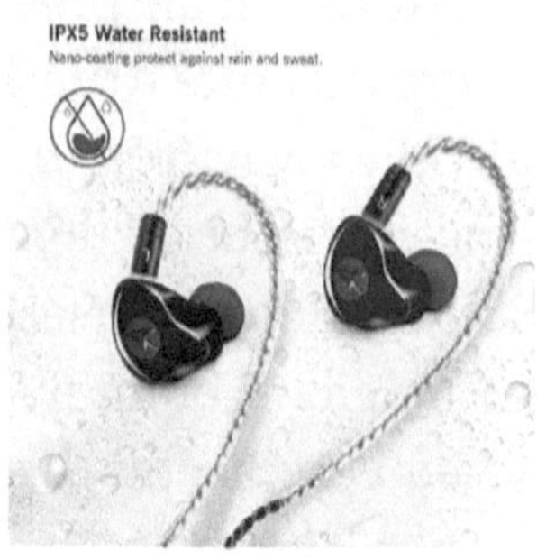

Unobtrusive In-ear Monitors

They don't pop out on screen as much as the larger Sennheisers, but they don't tunnel the sound as well. They do help to isolate sounds, and they can be adjusted to fit quite well, which is a problem that many other earbuds have failed badly at.

1080p Webcam

So, here's the deal. Logitech cameras have been difficult to locate since the entire planet got virtual because of COVID. A quality BRIO is also useful if you can find one and the seller isn't price gouging. However, because everyone is using Zoom these days, off-brand cameras are the way to go.

This webcam was recommended because it had numerous 5-star ratings. While it is possible to spoof Amazon's rating system, doing it 15,128 times is extremely difficult. Furthermore, the majority of the reviews are well-written and thorough, implying that this has real utility.

Option on a budget: Your laptop and phone both have cameras. Make use of them to save money. There is also some software on the google appstore that can turn your smartphone into a webcam. *Iriun* and *iVCam* are two of the popular choices.

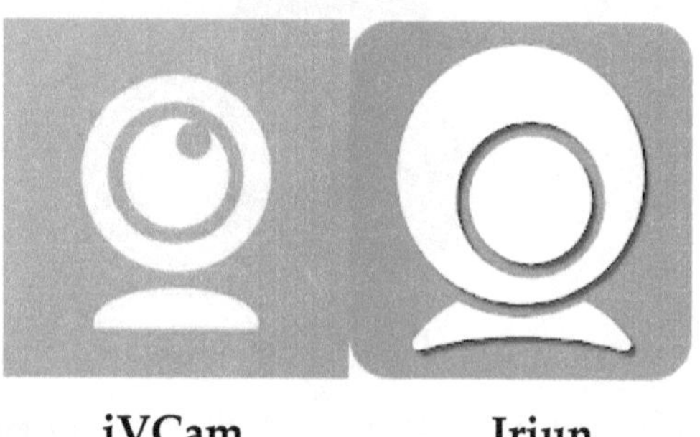

iVCam   Iriun

This tripod has adjustable-height and is made of lightweight aluminium; weighs just over a pound.

Basic Tripod

Tripods seemed to be popular during pandemics. All you need is a basic tripod if all you are supporting is a webcam (and potentially a lightweight teleprompter).

This one is perfect. It has a quick-release camera mount and quick release legs. It includes a smartphone adapter and a carrying case.

<u>Budget option:</u> This tripod is reasonably priced on its own, but if you want to go simple, stack a stack of books. Tape your camera to the back of a chair or a folding ladder. It's hot glued to a shelf. Persons have tried them all, and they work. Just not as easily as a tripod.

Acoustic Panels

Acoustic panels are one of many possibilities for muffled sound, but they should get you started.

Budget alternatives include raiding your attic and linen closet. Find old moving blankets, comforters, fuzzy blankets, or anything soft that can be used to muffle the noise.

Blackout Curtains

This elegant design two panels per package Blackout Curtain Panel measures 42 inches wide x 63 inches long. The NICETOWN drapery is constructed with rod pocket, fitting the curtain rod of your choice up to 2 inches in diameter, making the curtains easy to install and slide.

Blackout curtains can be as expensive as acoustic panels, but since they are so hefty, they are excellent sound buffers. They also shut out the light.

Teleprompter

This teleprompter comes with a large screen, the reflective screen measures 28cm x 19cm (TV studio size) and enables comfortable reading for the eyes. You can still read your text nicely from 5-6 meters.

It also has multi-device compatibility. The teleprompter kit is compatible with any smartphone (including smartphone holders), tablets, photo cameras, video cameras and can be mounted on all types of tripods.

With the reliable software along with the in-house developed projection software voice-teleprompter and the remote control from Leeventi you get everything from one place.

While teleprompters are excellent for reading scripts without glancing away from the camera. For a paltry amount, you may get a green screen, lighting, and stands.

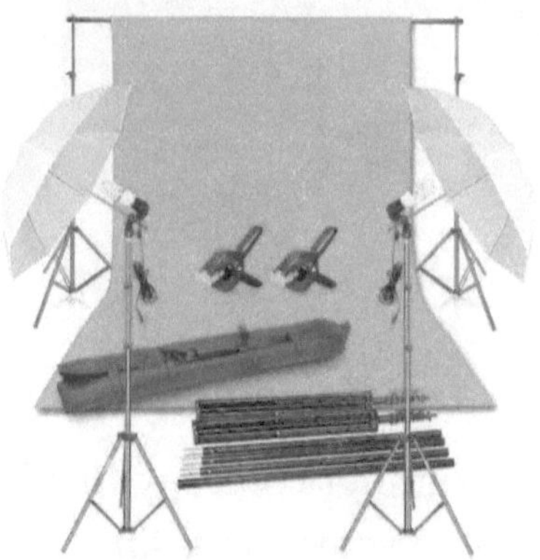

Green Screen Kit

This is an up-your-game improvement, but if you can't control your background and want to look professional, and you can pull off the lighting, a green screen may be the way to go. This kit is an excellent value. It comes with everything you'll need, including lights and a stand. The only issue is that it may require a little more space than you have available.

<u>Budget option</u>: You can also go with a simple background made up of items found around the house. There's no need to deal with all the lighting and positioning issues if you can simply carve out an area with a strong on-camera look.

For incorporating multiple video sources Blackmagic Design Blackmagic ATEM is deal.

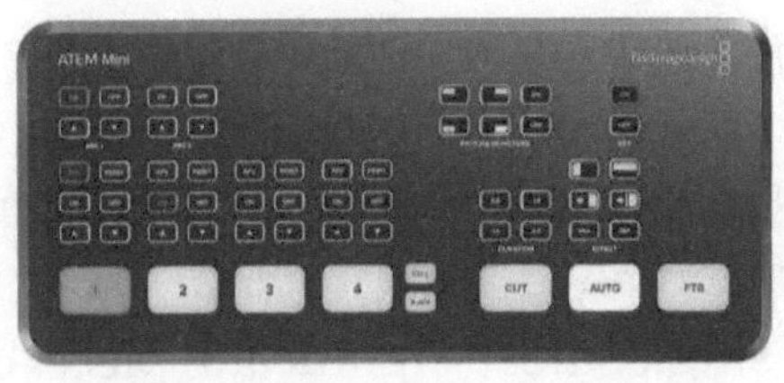

Blackmagic ATEM Mini

Consider the $295 ATEM Mini if you want to outsource your green screen processing from your computer to something with a lot of chromakey smarts. This is the first in a series of ATEM Mini devices that offload professional video production to small boxes that may run your home studio.

Unfortunately, Amazon has sold out of the $595 ATEM Mini Pro at the time this book was published, which offers live streaming (and is also subject to price gouging by scalpers, so be careful). Black Magic Design, the storied video gear company behind the ATEM line, has also just announced two cool new products: the $885 ATEM Mini Pro ISO, which has built-in individual multi-stream recording capabilities, and the ATEM Streaming Bridge, which converts the ATEM stream back into professional video formats.

<u>Budget option</u>: Simply use *OBS* on your computer to conduct all the processing and mixing. OBS is free, open-source, extremely powerful, and always improving.

The single most significant piece of equipment in the studio is scotch tape

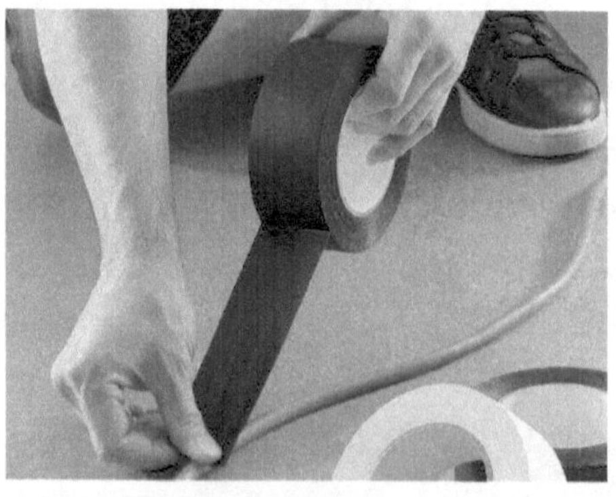

Gaffer Tape

You're in for a treat if you've never used gaffer tape. This substance is potent, yet does not leave a residue. It can be used in place of clamps and brackets, and it allows you to create temporary yet permanent mounts for your equipment. Taped a camera to a ladder with gaffer tape to simulate a tripod. Taped down all the cords for your lighting with gaffer tape.

Now that we have covered hardware, let's look at some useful software options to help make the teaching-learning process online flow more smoothly.

CHAPTER THREE:

The Best Remote Instructional Resources

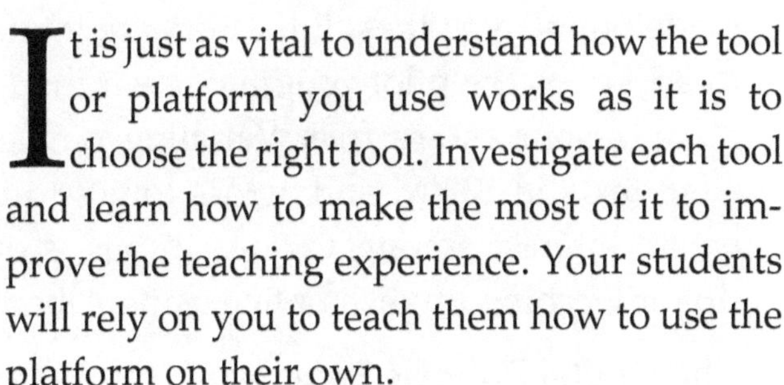

"We need technology in every classroom and in every student and teacher's hand, because it is the pen and paper of our time, and it is the lens through which we experience much of our world."– **David Warlick**

It is just as vital to understand how the tool or platform you use works as it is to choose the right tool. Investigate each tool and learn how to make the most of it to improve the teaching experience. Your students will rely on you to teach them how to use the platform on their own.

There is a variety of remote teaching software available, these are some of the finest ones they are classified based on their primary purpose.

Collaborate with your coworkers

Even if you don't see your coworkers every day in the corridor, they're still one of the most useful resources you have. It's easy to feel lonely while working from home, but don't be afraid to call out and inquire about what your coworkers are up to in their virtual classrooms. They're all doing the same thing you are: exploring and testing new tactics and technologies and sharing your findings is beneficial to everyone.

Meet your curricula's requirements

Albert has interesting, standards-aligned resources across all levels and subjects if you need to enhance your curriculum with ready-made online activities. Educators are invited to apply for the pilot program, even though many resources are free. Variating our levelled texts in STEM and across topics to increase interest among various pupils is one tip for teaching English online using Albert.

The Digital Promise Framework for EdTech

This method assists educational leaders in identifying and implementing effective educational technology pilots in their schools. The phases include identifying a need, finding and selecting a product, training employees, and more. Albert's pilot program adheres to many of these pilot principles, which is why schools that try us out first have a high rate of adoption and fidelity.

Always give a new tool a trial run before using it in class

Create a dummy class to allocate work to after you've decided which new tool to try. Log in and try out your activity as a student to see if it will work in your classroom. You'll also be able to assist with the troubleshooting of frequent issues you might not have spotted with only your instructor log-in.

Tools for Online Communication

Effective communication is essential for effective teaching and learning, whether in a physical or virtual classroom. Maintaining online communication with not one, but twenty pupils is difficult.

Communication systems assist in overcoming it by allowing communication with bigger groups, as well as video conferencing, instant messaging, voice conversations, virtual rooms, and other features, from any device and from anywhere.

Some of the tools in high demand are,

- MS Teams

- Zoom.

- Skype

- Google Meet

To improve your teaching experience with these tools,

- Make an agenda or a plan for each online class and share it with the class before the lecture.

- Explain clearly what internet etiquette students should use during the class and what is expected of them before or at the start of the course.

- All microphones should be muted except for the person speaking. This helps to drown out distracting noises and keep students focused. Anyone who needs to speak can make a gesture to get the speaker's attention without interrupting them.

- Allow time for students to take notes, see or go through them when presenting a presentation or sharing an image, document, or allow time for students to take notes, see or go through them when presenting a presentation or sharing an image, document, or file.

Online Whiteboards

Online whiteboards or digital whiteboards assist students in simulating the classroom whiteboard/blackboard experience. Most of these applications provide an endless canvas with shape libraries for building various forms of diagrams, charts, graphs, and other sorts of visualization (i.e. creating posters, graphic organizers, etc.).

Creately Editor- Creately for Online Teaching Tools

Educators utilize Creately for a variety of objectives, including:

- As an online whiteboard where professors and students may work together to visualize ideas, concepts, and so on. Furthermore, students and teachers can interact via in-app video conferencing and track one other's modifications using real-time mouse tracking and change previews.

- Create a variety of diagrams and graphics (such as dichotomous key diagrams, graphic organizers, lesson plans, and so on) for presentations, lessons, and tasks.

•	Documents should be shared with students and coworkers for their input and feedback (with in-line comments)

Workplace Planning Instruments

Maintaining a work schedule is even more crucial while working from home; especially during stressful times, a consistent pattern can help you make the best use of your time. Time management and scheduling software such as Google Calendar and Calendly can help you streamline:

•	Making timetables for your online classes or personal use

•	Creating online class schedules and keeping everyone informed of dates and times.

•	Making appointments with parents and students; avoid booking the same time period twice.

- Invite parents, students, or coworkers to online events (i.e. webinars)

- Developing lesson plans and sharing them with students, administrators, and coworkers.

Social Media Channels

Social media platforms are an excellent way for instructors, students, and parents to remain in touch.

Channels such as Facebook, LinkedIn, and WhatsApp enable the development of exclusive communities or groups that teachers can use.

- Maintain communication and presence after online class hours

- Share and save crucial lesson-related material, presentations, and resources.

- Hold Q&A sessions.

- Encourage pupils to communicate with one another and interact with one another while studying or doing homework.

- Organize live events such as webinars (with Facebook or Instagram Live)

Document Management Software

Teachers must keep a plethora of documents regularly, ranging from test papers to lesson plans. It is critical to have a central spot to store, organize, and manage all of these documents to keep track of them effectively, especially if you are teaching remotely.

Tools like GSuite, MS Office, OneDrive, Dropbox, and Evernote make it easier to keep track of the documents you own.

- Keep all papers, data, and so on in the cloud so that you and your students can access them from any device, from any location.

- Documents should be neatly organized in appropriate folders and subfolders to make them easier to find.

- With a simple link or as a file, you may quickly share files and documents with everyone. On GSuite apps, you may also change the permission settings to Edit, View, or Suggesting mode.

- Edit and review documents with students, offer comments and ideas and monitor changes using version history.

Online Video Resources

Loom and YouTube are excellent online video tools for creating and sharing videos with your students. These tools can be used in a variety of ways;

- Make a video of your online lessons or lectures and share it with your students.

- Students can watch the videos again if they were absent or if they are revising for a test. You can even film the video before to the class and share it with the pupils while you are away.

- If you are teaching the same subject to multiple classes, you can save time by using a pre-recorded session.

- Encourage autonomous learning by providing students with pre-recorded video lessons. When pupils comprehend a concept on their own, their chances of understanding it better increase.

- Share connections to existing online video resources.

Online Quiz Creators

Quizzes are an excellent tool to assess a student's performance, whether you are teaching online or in a physical classroom. Online quiz creators make it simple to,

- Online evaluations can be created, formatted, and shared.

- Create answer sheets that will allow you to conveniently track and score each student's answers.

Starting with Google Forms, there are a plethora of free and paid online quiz creators. We can find here more useful online quiz creators.

Platforms for Online Homework

Keeping track of pupils' assignments is one of the most difficult aspects of teaching from home.

Homework can take several forms, including essays, speeches, and tests. To get students to submit their assignments, you can use a mixture of the platforms listed above.

- Google Docs — for essays and other forms of written work.

- For spoken assignments, use Zoom, Skype, or other video conferencing tools.

- For films and presentations, use Loom, YouTube, Prezi, or Google Slides.

- Google Classroom - Assign tasks, grade them, and offer feedback.

CHAPTER FOUR:

Top Tips for New Teachers

"The most profound words will remain unread unless you can keep the learner engaged. You can't see their eyes to know if they got it so ... say it, show it, write it, demo it and link it to an activity." - **James Bates**

Kristina Garcia's Golden Nuggets

If you are new to online teaching or you have been doing it for a while, you will find these six tips shared by Kristina Garcia, an experienced educator, on how to teach online.

These six tips are:

Your virtual classroom background- how to set it up for your online classes

Your Lighting-because that's very important

Your appearance-how you will present yourself to your students

Space-and how to use it effectively

Focus-make sure that you are focusing in your classroom

Sustainability-take care of yourself mentally and physically

Background

The main thing you should think about when it comes to your classroom background is that it should not look like you are in your home even though you probably are in your home. Let's make sure that your classroom looks like a classroom it doesn't need to be anything extravagant neither does it needs to be distracting. A plain solid colour that compliments you and your outfit will be very suitable.

I recommend you know you don't have to have a whole room dedicated to teaching you can just find a simple space to set up the main thing is you don't want it to look like your home like I said you should not have your nightstand in the background. You should not have your refrigerator door there you want to emulate the classroom the traditional classroom as much as possible.

Just keep in mind that it doesn't have to be a huge space maybe like 4 or 6, you don't know square feet you just need a little space for online teaching which is pretty awesome

Lighting

It doesn't matter how great your background

is if they can't see your background. This is where lighting comes in. The best lighting you can ever have is natural light so if you are fortunate enough to be near a window and as a lot of sunshine where you live you are in luck that's not always the case for everybody most of us will need to supplement the lighting in some way even if you have a nice window you probably will need to supplement your lighting. But before you run out and buy any light it is recommended that you use whatever lighting you already have in your home.

Before you start your classes, you should test your lighting. Pull it up on your computer webcam using your camera app or Zoom, there is a free version of Zoom that you can use to test. This way you get to see how it would look and then recruit some help if there's somebody who can help you one of you stays in front of the camera and the other is moving around lights and lamps and trying to figure out what works.

Here are the top tips for getting those lamps to work for you. You want to be sure that you are bouncing lights from different directions and testing them out until you figure out what works best for your setting.

Appearance

Lighting is important because it highlights you so let's talk about you and your appearance.

For some female teachers, it may feel vain to be putting on makeup and trying to look good on camera but it helps to engage your student. It also helps you catch their attention. Using a headset is awesome because it masks bad hair days very nicely, so I typically don't worry too much about my hair when I'm teaching as long as it doesn't look crazy you might be okay getting away with maybe not doing quite as much with your hair. Maybe you like to do traditionally but besides your hair, another thing the students will see a lot of is your shirt so the best tip I can give you for your shirt is, of course, you want them to be modest because even more than usual there's going to be a lot of focus on your upper body. This is because there's not a whole lot more else to look at. You want your shirt to be modest and also a solid colour.

Why do we care about having a solid colour because not only is it less distressing for your students but it's less distracting for your webcam too.

Sometimes if you have polka dots or floral or stripes or something your webcam has a hard time focusing and it will go in and out of focus on you so wear a solid colour.

You can also wear a solid colour lipstick if you are so inclined and you feel up to it I encourage you to consider wearing lipstick in your classes this is especially helpful because for your students who read lips. Your lips are going to be so much smaller on the screen right in supposing that some of your students will rely on reading your lips highlight it with just a little bit of colour.

The other makeup that I would recommend if you want to wear makeup is some eyeliner this will help draw attention to your eyes so let's talk about.

Let's talk about eye contact because it is even more important in the online classroom than you would ever imagine. The top concern I hear from most teachers about eye contact is I have no clue where to look and I understand that because when you're face-to-face with a student in person you look at your student directly. With a webcam, I encourage you 99% of the time you want to be looking in one of these two places either directly at your webcam or scan your virtual classroom.

Here you are probably wondering what that 1% is where else you might be looking occasionally you will need to look at your video just to make sure that you are still within the screen, just to ensure your video is working but most of the time you want to be looking at your webcam for your students.

Space

If you're not looking at your students directly, if you're not looking at the web then you might need to be checking to make sure that you are within your space so let's talk about space.

The worst thing that you can do with your space is put everything on top of each other for example if I'm trying to hold up a prop in front of the camera you don't want to cover or block your face while you are trying to teach. Doing this make the students disengage because they can't see you anymore but you can't see your students either.

I have another quick fix to that problem it's another four-letter letter word, it is *lean*. You just want to lean I know that this seems super simple but you want to lean and you want to share the space left to right. Don't just think about your space left to right I want you to think about your space close and far from the webcam so for example, a time when you might want to get up close to your webcam as if you're pronouncing something for your student or maybe you are singing to them or maybe they are not paying attention and you just want to get their attention real quick so you go in. There are times when would you will need to go far maybe if you have something big you want to show right now if you want to do a gesture, or if you are trying to use using that space moving front-to-back and side-to-side keeps your students engaged and it helps them to focus a lot more.

Focus

Let's talk about focus. Not only is it helpful to think about how your students can focus better but also how you can help them focus better.

As the teacher, one of the most distressing things for online teachers; at least from what I've experienced and heard from other teachers is noises so you want to minimize noises in your classroom and your home in general. Of course, you wouldn't want to throw a load of laundry in if you're near the laundry machine the washing machine anything like that so you want to minimize any kind of mechanical noises if you have an overhead fan of the noisy variety you want to turn it off. I'm sorry you may be a little toasty but you probably don't want to do that and then you want to avoid anything that distracts or take away from the teaching-learning experience.

I got a doorbell and ringing it is distracting. Now I put a sign on my doorbell I don't put it next to my doorbell I put it on the doorbell so that the UPS driver or whoever cannot even use the doorbell because i cover it up. You want to put a sign just to let people know not to make noise outside the door and the door to your classroom.

If you live with any other people you want to be sure that they know the expectation that when you are teaching, they do not come in and ask you for juice or they don't barge in just to ask what you're doing.

You know the people you live with better than I do but I know a lot of teachers who will put a sign on their door like a stop sign. One of the teachers who I know and love put a picture of Grumpy Cat on his door to let his parents know not to go in so whatever works. Some people and critters who will not respond even if you put up a sign maybe they can't read it or they just don't understand. So for them, you just need to get into some kind of routine maybe somebody needs to help you with that just making sure that that person or critter is not coming in during your classes.

I know some teachers will sometimes have their pets in their classroom with them I used to be one of them and here's why I'm no longer one of them. One time I was teaching in my class and I had a very young kitten and he would sleep on my feet during classes and then one day all of a sudden, I was teaching and he crawled up my back and pop cross and sit upon my shoulder like a parrot in the middle of class. I never thought that he would do that so sometimes those are the sneaky ones so you just want to be careful about any kind of distractions that could distract you and then ultimately distract your students.

Sustainability

We don't know how long this teaching online

will last for so we want to focus also on sustainability. What do I mean by that? I mean that you need to be sure you're taking care of yourself so you don't burn out just like how teachers can burn out in the traditional classroom I've seen good teachers burn out in the online classroom too.

What can we do about that? You want to hydrate – drink a lot of water. Hydration is so important when I was a new teacher online after the first two weeks or so I completely lost my voice and I think it's because I wasn't hydrating and I wasn't focused on my vocal health. Focus on your vocal Health are lots of great products out there that can help you know that have different natural products. I encourage you to take good care of yourself or you will burn out you will I don't want that for you.

One bonus tip

Give yourself grace especially if you've never taught in the online classroom before this is overwhelming, it is and you are a champ and you're going to do fine but you need to take care of yourself.

Be easy on yourself. You will drop things; you may accidentally turn off your webcam for a while you may have no clue how to manage your classroom you know they're there are so many things that could come up but ultimately, I encourage you to remind yourself why got you into teaching in the first place.

I bet it's the passion that brought you there and that passion doesn't just extinguish because now you're online, so I encourage you to keep doing what you do and passionately teaching the students.

I'm avoiding software advice because teachers require a wide range of software, much of which is prescribed by the school district. Teachers, on the other hand, require students to have access to computers and bandwidth, and there is a significant digital gap.

Now that we have covered these essential tips, let look at how to plan your lessons for online teaching.

CHAPTER FIVE:

How to Plan an Effective Online Lesson

"The illiterate of the 21st century will not be those who cannot read and write, but those who cannot learn, unlearn, and relearn."– Alvin Toffler

Most EdTech discussions revolve around "tech" new apps, data systems, assessments, and other technology. However, debates about education, particularly the art of teaching with these instruments, are frequently inadequate.

Master educators have expressed their frustration at the difficulty of translating in-person teaching concepts to different media. With this in mind, here are a few pointers for online teaching.

In tips, 1 to 6 actionable ideas are offered for your use when planning and designing an online course.

1. Make Use Of Lesson Plan Templates

When creating an online course, one of the

most frequently ask is, "Where do I begin?" To begin, a great recommendation is to use an online lesson design template developed by other educators who have a thorough understanding of the online teaching space. This will help you give structure to the process. "Who will take this course?" and "What are my learning objectives?" are two useful questions to ask. This data can help you make all of the future design decisions you'll need to make when you build your course.

2. Determine Component Skills

Consider the time when you were learning to drive. You had to learn to master and then combine component skills such as changing lanes, deciphering street signals, and applying brakes, among others. Other undertakings, such as learning to play the piano or mastering math, can be broken down into component abilities.

When creating a course outline for online teaching, it is recommended that you identify the component abilities that your students will need to learn to master the subject. You can then construct an environment in which the student can practice those abilities individually before learning to integrate them.

3. Get Your Learner Involved

Students sign up for many online courses a few weeks before the session officially begins. This means you may have access to prospective students' email addresses while constructing the course.

Involving those learners in the course design process might be accomplished by asking them about their course objectives. You can next evaluate the themes that emerged from the replies and incorporate the student-generated learning objectives into your lesson planning. According to research, "when instructors identify and reinforce poor component abilities through targeted practice," student performance improves significantly.

4. Investigate Misconceptions And Debates

"What misconceptions do my students have about the material?" expert teachers inquire. Some even set up a pre-test to induce such misunderstandings. The next design situations inside their course in which students are confronted with such assumptions. It is recommended that you include this question in your list of items to consider when preparing for the course.

Expert teachers also wonder, "Whose voices,

other than mine, do the kids need to hear?" They encourage debate and invite outside lecturers to present students with fresh ideas.

One excellent example is Barbara Oakley's online course "Learning How To Study," in which she advises on how to learn more successfully and then interviews guest speakers who have mastered those skills.

5. Create A Great Course Prototype

Once you've decided on the learner and learning objectives for your online course, you'll probably make many design decisions based on the activities you want your students to participate in.

While developing your course, I propose that you request input on such activities from representative learners. A useful resource to examine here is the framework provided by Stanford University's School of Engineering, which can assist you in gathering feedback from learners while employing low-fidelity prototypes.

This way of gathering input early in the design process can aid in the sharpening of learning activities.

Another advantage of prototype testing is that it will assist you in identifying expert blind spots in your course. Expert blind spot is defined by learning scientists as the incapacity of some instructors to make correct predictions about the difficulty level of new ideas as perceived by their students. In other words, specialists are sometimes unable to recollect what it is like to be a rookie and are oblivious of the challenges that a rookie faces with their field. Prototype testing the course at the design stage can assist you in identifying such trouble locations.

6. Create Emotionally Satisfying Content

Here's a question for you: What do you consider to be the features of a well-designed product? This product could be a phone, a website, or a web-based course.

Don Norman, the author of Emotional Design, contends that well-designed objects are not only highly useful but also emotionally satisfying.

Consider a simple coffee cup. Now the cup must fulfill its principal function, which is to hold a hot beverage. If it didn't, we'd all assume it was poorly designed. However, this alone does not take the cup to the level of well-designed. To do this, the cup must also be emotionally rewarding to the user. One way the designer can achieve this is by making grooves in the cup's handle that allow the coffee user to comfortably place her fingers.

The main lesson we can learn from designers (of wonderful phones, cups, and vehicles) as teachers is to ask ourselves, "Is this activity or presentation emotionally rewarding for my students?"

Teaching An Effective Online Course
Tips 7 through 10, which highlight techniques that will help you teach more effectively in an online space.

7. Provide Early Victories

Efficacy is a huge term, but its impact on a student's capacity to learn something new is much enormous. Simply defined, self-efficacy relates to a student's belief in her ability to succeed in a new scenario.

Numerous studies have shown that self-efficacy beliefs have a significant impact on a student's academic progress. For example, research indicates that students who have a strong belief in their abilities to solve math problems outperform those who have concerns. Furthermore, students who express high levels of self-efficacy stay in technical majors longer than those who do not.

One strategy to assist learners in developing efficacy is to provide them with early wins in your online lectures. A little task at the start of the course can assist students to gain confidence. Susan Ambrose proposes in her book, How Learning Works, that this method is especially useful in "gateway or high-risk courses."

8. Make Use Of Prior Knowledge

Our students are not empty canvases. They bring prior experiences to a lesson that can either help or impede the learning process. Unsurprisingly, educational research shows that learning occurs when students relate new concepts to prior information or experiences. In light of this, the following question should be considered when developing an online course: What do my students already know about this subject? It might also be a good idea to do a preliminary test to identify this information. You can then draw attention to students' prior knowledge and use their responses to create opportunities for new learning.

9. Contrast And Compare

Some of the approaches outlined here may have been influenced by the actions of an expert teacher in a physical classroom. The advice to "compare and contrast" has a similar foundation.

Expert teachers frequently inspire their students to study by pointing out the distinctions and similarities between various concepts. These concepts could be two distinct arguments, two pieces of code that perform the same function but are written in separate programming languages, or two approaches to the same problem. According to research, this type of comparing thinking can result in significant learning gains and can aid in the transfer of knowledge from one scenario to another.

10. Make Use Of Silence

If you ever find yourself using Skype or Google Hangout to teach in real-time, you might want to think about creating silent places for pupils to contemplate.

Expert teachers, in my experience, will identify times when they want their students to think separately about specific issues. One of my graduate school instructors used to use this method in his lectures regularly. "I want you to take a minute to enjoy the stillness and reflect on the major theme from last week's paper," he would add.

Many other teachers will schedule ample class time for all pupils to consider a topic or prompt before requesting comments, preventing one person from blurting out the answer. This methodology is based on the Think, Pair, Share concept, which is used by teachers all around the world to facilitate dialogues.

This method also works effectively when posing questions to students. Instead of asking if there are any questions, I advocate giving students 30 seconds to write down any unanswered questions before sharing them with the rest of the class. Silence can also be used effectively in asynchronous courses with pre-recorded videos. Include scenarios in your video content where you urge students to pause and reflect at critical times before continuing with the course.

We've reached the halfway mark of this four-part blog series. In my next post, I'll discuss techniques for helping your students connect with and learn from one another. Then I'll see you!

Building Community For Your Online Course

Learning online may be a very isolating experience. You sit at your computer, working for the most part in a secluded digital island, oblivious to your classmates' troubles in the course. In this piece, I'd like to discuss some strategies for connecting online students and building a lively learning community.

However, before we proceed, review the ten guidelines I listed in prior postings on how to organize and teach an online course.

11. Demonstrate Student Diversity

Creating a sense of community in an online classroom is a huge task. Students in an online situation, in my experience, may not get to know each other as well as their counterparts in a real classroom, and so may not feel inspired to work with and aid one another.

To foster community, I like to offer my students a survey at the start of the course that collects information on their academic backgrounds and hobbies. In a recent online coding course, I added the following survey question: "How confident do you feel in your ability to program?"

I then post the survey findings on the discussion topic. I'm guessing the following are some of the effects of your class: 42 percent of you have a humanities background; 89 percent are scared by programming, and 12 percent have juggling as a special interest.

Now, I admit that the percentages given above will fluctuate for your online course, but this effort will disclose the diverse nature of your class to your students and try to make the learners identify with their peers.

12. Liven Up The Forums

Conversations in an online course typically take place in a discussion forum. Here are a few things I've attempted to foster a vibrant forum community.

Instead of presenting questions with a single perfect answer, I offer open-ended questions that encourage students to draw on their personal experiences to produce several alternative responses. For example, in an iPhone programming class, I asked my students to choose their favorite app and describe its various architectural components.

Quora is a question-and-answer website where users pose intriguing queries such as "How painful is heart surgery?" What makes Quora even more intriguing is that the best answers are usually provided by people who have some knowledge of the subject. For example, one of the most popular answers to the question about heart surgery was written by someone who had a triple bypass.

You can mimic this idea in your discussion boards by inviting professors/experts to share their thoughts. I requested Oliver Cameron, an iOS expert who built an app that was number one on the app store in 2009, to remark on one of the forums in a course on iPhone app creation. Oliver's post was the most liked in the thread.

Set aside some time to answer queries on the forums to help establish a community. Students are more inclined to participate if the instructor takes the time to answer some of their inquiries.

If you're teaching an online class with a big number of students, you might notice that certain forum discussions have hundreds of responses. While such participation is wonderful, a high number of replies on a discussion thread might make it difficult for students to understand the broad themes or specific discoveries. In such cases, you may find it useful to "pin" or designate a few responses that you want all students in the class to read.

13. Link Students

In 2013, MIT and Harvard researchers published a study in which they reviewed data obtained from Circuits and Electronics, to find student habits that led to academic performance.

According to one key conclusion in this survey, "a student who worked offline with someone else in the class or someone who had experience in the subject would have a forecasted score nearly three points higher than someone working alone."

This research highlights the importance of collaboration in student learning. As a result, I recommend you use tools like Meetup.com to encourage students enrolled in your online course to locate and collaborate with other students in their area.

Talkabout is another tool that uses video chat

software to link pupils. This application, designed in collaboration with academics from UC San Diego and Stanford University, uses video chat to connect a group of students taking an online course and helps assist their dialogue by delivering prompts produced by course designers. According to a recent study, involvement in these discussion groups boosted student performance on course assignments by half a letter grade.

14. Give Feedback

To encourage engagement and conversation in your online classroom, offer open-ended questions. Inquiries such as "How would you tackle this problem?" as well as "What is the flaw in this piece of work?"

Such inquiries function particularly effectively in a typical classroom setting, where a teacher can provide specific feedback on these discoveries. However, in an online world, the task of understanding and responding to paragraph-sized open-ended comments remains an unsolved technical problem. This is probably one of the main reasons why multiple-choice questions abound in online courses.

Now, I must say that I am optimistic about

employing artificial intelligence software to read long form responses: a Microsoft Research technology appears to be promising, and a learning platform called Oppia seeks to deliver unique feedback. However, these are still a long way from being widely used in online courses.

An alternative option could be to provide feedback in the form of curated, exemplary peer responses. In one of my online courses, I ask students to divide a huge problem into smaller parts and then submit their answers into a textbox. After the learner clicks submit, I provide comment on a previous response given by another student in the course. As a result, the learner will be able to compare their proposal to an outstanding solution that I have selected.

Desmos, a math education startup, used a similar strategy in one of their math projects to highlight peer replies as feedback.

I believe this method is worth trying if a lack of response to open-ended questions is preventing you from employing such inquiries in your online course.

15. Seek Feedback

Some of the top teachers, in my opinion, solicit anonymous input from their pupils on how they may improve their teaching approach and substance. I recommend that you perform an online survey to collect student feedback anywhere in the first half of the course and then use that data to improve the rest of the course.

Vanderbilt University's Center for Teaching offers a wonderful foundation for conducting surveys that might assist in obtaining student feedback.

In the fourth and last instalment of this four-part blog series, I'll go over how to use evaluations as a learning tool in an online course. Then I'll see you.

Using Physical Space & Assessments in Your Online Course

Learning in an online setting can be hampered by a small screen that does not fully utilize a student's physical area. In this final session, we will look at how to incorporate the learner's hands, physical environment, and experiences into the learning process.

16. Identify The Learner's Location

The online courses I've created necessitate an

investment of up to 20 hours from the learner. This means that the learner may need several days or even weeks to complete the course. It is also critical to provide students with a map of their current placement in the course, as well as an indication of the progress they have made and the road ahead.

I utilized stairs as a metaphor for advancement in one of my courses to help students answer the question, "Where am I in the class?" With each class, I climbed up the stairs to offer the learner a new "you are here location."

This course map functions similarly to a table of contents in a book; it assists the learner in locating her own progress.

17. Investigate The Following Episode

Online courses are frequently made up of numerous lessons or modules. Asking students to reflect on the new ideas they have learnt is a terrific approach to end each class.

Another interesting strategy for providing a preview for impending information at the end of a class is to provide a teaser for the next topic. This may encourage pupils to continue learning or set aside time to return.

18. Make Use Of Hand Gestures And Space

Embedded cognition, as defined by psychologists, shows us that a student's ability to learn and recall new ideas is influenced by his bodily experiences. For example, studies show that when people utilize improvisation to physically play out a story, they remember it more than when they simply read or debate the story with others.

Incorporating the learner's hands, surrounding space, and different sensory abilities into the learning process can be especially challenging in an online setting where the student is on the other end of the fibre-optic line, attempting to learn by watching a video or reading some text.

Prof. David Malan of Harvard University used this method well while teaching his programming students how to sort a sequence of numbers. He called eight pupils to the stage, assigned each of them a number, and then instructed them to change spots as decided by a sorting algorithm. When describing how computer programs function in an online course, I tried to use space in a similar way.

When making videos for your course, I encourage pushing the video frame's boundaries and interacting with the physical space around you. In my opinion, pupils can better internalize knowledge when they can relate to their lecturers' bodily actions.

19. Turning Students Become Teachers

"Teach it to someone else if you actually want to learn it." This was the last piece of advice my computer science lecturer gave to graduating students. The relevance of this phrase became clear to me only after I began working as a middle school science teacher; when I investigated themes with my pupils, the gaps in my understanding were revealed.

I encouraged my online learners to become teachers in order to assist them in understanding the gaps in their knowledge. At the end of a project, I encouraged my students to teach what they had learned to a friend; I also asked them to capture photos or videos of the event and post their experiences on the discussion forum.

This effort resulted in thousands of posts and ten times the number of views. One of the most touching anecdotes came from Maria, a student in Montreal, who talked about her program with her partner, and another from

Qamardeen, who wanted to teach his wife how to code.

While these stories were extremely fulfilling for me as a teacher, they were also an excellent learning tool for my students. Educational researchers have found that pupils who are aware that they must teach a subject to someone else learn more than those who are merely learning for themselves. The "protege effect" properly describes this phenomenon.

My suggestion is that you urge students in your online course to share what they've learned with someone they know.

20. Compose Blogs And One-Minute Papers

Purdue University researchers discovered that students who recollect and write new ideas after reading a body of text remember and grasp the ideas much better than those who just re-read the same text numerous times.

Expert instructors employ writing as a tool to increase learning in a variety of ways, including the One-Minute Paper technique, which educators refer to as retrieval practice. This is how it works: Near the close of the lesson, the teacher instructs her students to write down their responses to the following two questions:

What key concepts did you learn in class today? What are your thoughts on today's lesson? To accomplish this in your online class, at the end of each lesson, ask students to summarize important topics and indicate any unsolved questions. This exercise assists your students in assessing their knowledge while also providing you with statistics on popular student questions you can use to improve your course.

I attempted a variation of this strategy by having my pupils write blogs. I allowed my students to write about the new ideas they uncovered in the course three-quarters of the way through an online course on creating an iPhone app. I highlighted some of the top blogs on the course website to encourage students to complete this task.

We have now reached the end of this four-part blog series in which I attempted to contribute to the discussion on how to teach more effectively in an online environment. Have you discovered any other ways that can aid in creating effective online learning experiences? I invite you to leave your ideas in the comments section below.

CHAPTER SIX:

Planning an Effective Online Course

"The most effective, successful professionals are constantly learning, they take the time to apply what they have learned, and they continually work to improve themselves." - Joel Gardner

Why Online Learning Isn't Going Away

There is no such thing as perfection, and online learning does not solve all of a school's challenges. Traditional, brick-and-mortar classrooms, on the other hand, cannot suit the needs of a wide range of kids and school districts.

Fully virtual schools have been springing up all across the globe for years, and their popularity is only growing. While some families have discovered that full-time distant learning does not fit their lifestyles, it is necessary for others. To mention a few, there are competitive student-athletes with strict training schedules, students with mental or physical illnesses, and families who simply desire more flexibility in their day.

For their in-person audiences, even traditional schools are using virtual courses. Consider a district that wishes to offer a cinema studies course to its students but lacks the resources or student numbers to warrant hiring a full-time film teacher in each building. Instead, this district will hire a single teacher to teach the course digitally using an online Learning Management System like Canvas or Moodle. This virtual course is now available to students throughout the district at any time during the day in their school's computer lab. Virtual tools, digital subscriptions, practice software, and Internet are all being invested in by schools. Digital citizenship classes are becoming more popular as part of school curricula.

It might be challenging for educators who are new to distance learning to know what online teaching approaches perform best, or even where to start. Some excellent online teaching tactics are outlined, provide easy-to-use advice, and present several accessible resources.

The Keys to Effective Online Class Teaching
While everyone's teaching approach is a little different, great online instructors all adhere to

the same best practices. All of the best online learning tactics are built on these five simple concepts.

1. Maintain Open Lines Of Communication With Your Students' Families

Families expect to hear from you frequently and regularly. It's all too simple for students and parents to get disengaged. Reassure them that your "virtual door" is always open, and provide them with your email and phone number in several places early and often. Building relationships and a sense of community in the classroom requires clear, respectful communication.

Prepare students and families for a successful year, communicate your expectations and due dates early and regularly using interesting communications such as weekly newsletters and personal phone calls.

2. Vary The Kind Of Lessons You Teach.

Your lessons should be a mix of synchronous (real-time) and asynchronous (non-real-time) (unscheduled and self-paced). Students can ask questions and form relationships with you and each other through synchronous instruction via phone calls, video courses, or live chats. Students can complete coursework at their own pace with asynchronous activities like discussion boards or recorded lectures. Both approaches have advantages and are necessary in their own right.

3. *Choose The Appropriate Tools For Your Class.*

Find and use the most appropriate EdTech for your needs. Select and apply the finest resources for your classroom, collaborate with other educators and identify unique needs. The Learning Management System (LMS) in your school will most likely be the primary tool you utilize for direct contact and assignment publishing. Familiarize yourself with it as soon as possible, and don't be afraid to ask your more tech-savvy colleagues questions. You'll also need different technology for phone conversations, live courses, and video chat, such as Google Voice, Google Meet or Zoom.

4. *Adapt Your Teachings To Operate In An Online Environment.*

Engaging dialogues, screen recordings, and interactive tech tools can help you transform your in-person lectures into an online environment.

5. Create A Supportive Online Classroom Environment.

In the virtual classroom, classroom community is just as important, and it may be built through video chats, purposeful free time, and class message boards.

Aside from these fundamentals, there are a plethora of educational technology solutions available to help you transform your teaching and engage your students. This is one of the most enjoyable parts of online teaching! You have so much to discover, experiment with, and integrate into your classroom to enhance the teaching-learning experience.

How to Adapt Your Lesson Plans to Different Types of Learners:

We know you've already spent many hours adjusting and improving your lesson plans. Don't feel as if your hard effort has been in vain! You can alter your in-person lesson ideas to meet the virtual setting using a variety of online learning tactics. All it takes is a little imagination and the correct tools.

6. Increase Engagement And Comprehension By Including Dialogues.

Flipgrid is an unequalled tool for asynchronous discussions. Instead of typing, students film themselves responding to the questions you've provided. They can also watch and respond to each other's videos. This is an excellent alternative for reluctant writers, as well as a powerful tool to increase interest and encourage active learning.

Google Classroom is a fantastic tool for written discussions. Simply post the assignment instructions, allow students to publish their responses, and then allow them to read and reply to other student's responses.

Students can message back and forth in real-time in chat rooms like YO Teach for synchronous discussions. Fair warning: active instructor monitoring is required in these chatrooms.

7. Pre-Record Yourself And Your Classes Using Screen Recordings.

Screen recording software like *Loom* or *Screencastify* allows you to record your presentation on-screen as you speak and scroll through your slides for the PowerPoint you've already produced. It also allows you to add a little window with your face on the screen so that your pupils can see you. These videos are available for download or sharing via a web-link.

You can also video yourself explaining assignment directions for pupils that learn best when they are instructed what to do verbally.

8. Make Your Lessons Fun And Participatory

One approach to make online classes more participatory is to use *Nearpod*. It's a dynamic tool that lets students use their own devices to follow along with and participate in your lessons. You begin by importing your existing lesson pdfs or PowerPoint. Then you can include locations for students to interact, such as written responses, drawings, quizzes, polls, collaboration boards, and so on. You can tailor the type and difficulty of assignments to meet the needs of various students.

You may have the latest and best apps for teaching online but you still need to manage your classroom effectively to ensure your teaching objectives are achieved.

CHAPTER SEVEN:

Online Classroom Management Tips

"Research suggests that all students are motivated to learn, as long as there are clear expectations, the tasks and activities have value, and the learning environment promotes intrinsic motivation - **Wlodkowski & Ginsberg et al.**

Strong classroom management is just as important in an online setting as it is in a traditional setting. These class-wide and one-on-one classroom management strategies perform well across disciplines and grade levels. They should empower you to create an orderly yet welcoming and engaging atmosphere without the need for administrative or parental assistance. An online classroom with poor classroom management will almost assuredly elevate your stress and burnout rates.

Why is online classroom management vital?
Classroom management is important for three reasons. When done correctly:

- It creates and maintains order in the online classroom environment.

- It enhances meaningful academic learning and promotes social-emotional development

- It increases academic engagement and decreases negative classroom conduct in students

1. Model Excellent Behavior

Make it a habit to model the behaviour you want to see, as numerous studies show that modelling effectively teaches students how to act in various situations.

- Use courteous words.

- Make eye contact.

- Put away your phone.

- Allow each other to speak uninterrupted.

- Express your dissatisfaction with one another's statements respectfully.

2. Involve Students in Making Rules and Guidelines.

Encourage all students to assist you in developing online classroom expectations and regulations, as this will result in greater buy-in than simply telling them what they are not allowed to do.

Spend time in your first synchronous lesson discussing with your students what you want your "Online Classroom Norms" to be as a class. Make a list of approximately 8-10 standards, including specific guidelines like "remain on topic," "always be nice and respectful," and "raise your hand and wait to be called on before turning on your microphone." After you've made your list, go over it with your students and share it before each live session.

3. Write down the regulations.

Don't let your mutually agreed-upon guidelines fall by the wayside.

Disseminate the list of rules developed by the class discussion in the same way that you would a syllabus. Then, with your students, go over the list. This demonstrates your appreciation for their opinions and your intention to follow them. And if a student violates a rule, you'll be able to easily refer to this document.

If you're feeling particularly inventive, incorporate the rule list in a student handbook with crucial dates, events, and curricular material.

4. Try not to punish the class

Address isolated discipline issues individually rather than disciplining an entire class, as the latter might harm your relationships with on-task students and risk other classroom management initiatives.

Instead, politely, call out specific students. As an example:

"Do you have a question?" rather than "Stop talking and distracting other students."

"Do you need assistance focusing?" rather than "Pay attention and stop messing around while I'm talking."

This fundamental strategy will allow you to maintain a polite demeanour while promptly recognizing inappropriate behaviour.

5. Motivate initiative

Allow students to work ahead and offer brief presentations to provide takeaway points to promote a growth attitude and provide diversity to your courses. You will almost certainly have some eager students in your class.

Simply ask them whether they want to get forward from time to time. For example, if you're reading a specific chapter in a textbook, suggest that they also read the one after that. When they deliver their future presentations on your behalf to preview the following chapter, you may discover that other students want a bit more work as well.

6. Give compliments

According to a recent research review and study, rewarding students for good work enhances academic and behavioural performance.

When it is genuine and includes concrete examples of effort or achievement, praise can:

- Motivate the class

- Boost a student's self-esteem

- Make the rules and iideas you wish to see more of a priority.

Perhaps more crucially, it motivates children to engage in positive behaviour in the future. Assume a student demonstrates outstanding problem-solving abilities when attempting a math word problem. Praise for his or her usage of specific strategies should go a long way toward ensuring that he or she uses these strategies in the future. Not to mention that you will inspire other students to do the same.

7. Make use of nonverbal communication

A vigilant teacher supplementing her speech with tech signals to make students aware that they are being monitored frequently. For example, flipping thru windows to ensure all students are involved with the assigned class activity.

To improve material delivery, use actions and visual aids to help students focus and process teachings.

These communication approaches are the foundation of many differentiated instruction tactics and methodologies. Running learning stations, for example, allows you to present a variety of nonverbal content kinds by dividing your classroom into areas through which students circulate. Videos, infographics, and blogs are examples of this.

8. Make positive letters and phone calls

Keep students happy in and out of class by pleasantly surprising their parents, making positive phone calls and sending complimentary emails.

When the occasion arises, from academic effort or behavioural progress, letting parents know has a trickle-down effect. They'll generally congratulate their child; their child will likely come to class eager to earn more positive feedback. This can also entice parents to grow more invested in a child's learning.

9. Create enthusiasm for the subject and lesson preparations

A teacher appears on the screen to her class, attempting to pique students' interest by previewing fascinating aspects of the day's course.

This one work well in any grade level: elementary, middle school, or high school. Begin lessons by previewing particularly fascinating parts, piquing students' interest right away.

Go through an agenda of the day's highlights with the entire class. These could include collaborative tasks, interesting content, and anything else that piques your interest. For instance, "Throughout the period, you will study about:"

- How to Speak Like a Teacher (sentence structure)

- Why don't you know anyone who has won the lottery? (probability)

- What all of the United States presidents had in common (social analysis)

The purpose of this classroom management strategy is to immediately pique students' interest in your agenda and so deter misconduct.

10. Provide several sorts of free study time

Provide a variety of activities during free study time to appeal to students who struggle to comprehend knowledge alone in silence.

You can accomplish this by separating your class into clearly defined solo and online group activities. Consider the following in different sections:

- Providing audiobooks with material relevant to your lessons

- Making a chat or social media group for difficult group

activities that teach or reinforce curriculum-aligned skills

• Allowing students to work in groups while taking notes and completing assignments outside of the online class time.

By organizing these types of activities, free study time will begin to serve a wide range of students. This should help to increase overall classroom participation.

11. Assign unrestricted projects.

Encourage students to work on open-ended projects that do not require a precise product so that they can demonstrate their knowledge in ways that are natural to them.

To begin, distribute a list of broad project ideas to the class and invite each student to select one. Make sure to include a rubric that clearly explains expectations for each project. You should note that by appealing and challenging students:

• They can work and study at their own pace.

- Engage in active participation with suitable content

- Demonstrate knowledge as effectively as feasible

With these advantages, students may look forward to embarking on new initiatives.

12. Every live discussion should have conduct expectations

Especially in live discussions, make your rules/expectations extremely apparent from the start. Even the quieter kids will likely feel more confident posting in the chat, which is excellent when the dialogue is nice, but not so wonderful when it deviates from the topic or becomes improper.

13. In real-time debates, establish and enforce penalties

It's just as crucial to enforce your expectations as it is to set and express them in any classroom. You can simply silence or delete a student who is not actively engaging in the lecture. Then, following that, make a phone call to your family to discuss the matter.

14. Locate your source of positive reinforcement

Cleaning the whiteboard or receiving small pieces of candy are some students' favourite activities. However, these benefits do not apply online. However, rewarding students is still necessary to reinforce their good behaviour. Here are a few suggestions:

Star students should be recognized via emails to the class, during synchronous lessons, or on a student bulletin board. Students can even use a platform like Padlet to post shoutouts to each other.

Send personalised messages to students and their families when they've done a fantastic job. Allowing pupils to make even seemingly little decisions can be inspiring. Allow a student to select music to play before the start of the session, or select a humorous image for your virtual Zoom background.

15. Establish explicit deadlines

Many students have trouble managing their time. It's easy for them to lose track of time and fall behind on their work if they don't have a strict school day plan. Set deadlines for everything and give out reminders regularly. To assist students to stay on track, break down large assignments into smaller chunks wherever possible. Set a due date for the outline, the rough draft, and the final essay, for example, if you're assigned an essay. This encourages those who prefer to wait until the last minute to go forward at a steady pace. Another example for the art teachers, you can have your students submit photos or videos of the major stages of a project.

16. Take advantage of acknowledgement forms

In this internet world, you'll undoubtedly question, "Does anyone even read my emails?" Add a link to a brief Google Form where a student or parent may input their name to acknowledge they read and understood any very critical communications to ensure your children read and comprehend them.

CHAPTER EIGHT:

Building Rapport and Community Online

"The most important principle for designing lively eLearning is to see eLearning design not as information design but as designing an experience." - Cathy Moore

I t's tougher to connect on a human level with people when they exist in two dimensions on your computer screen or mobile device," according to a Forbes 2018 article titled *How to Build Real Relationships in the Virtual World*. You need to put in extra effort to ensure that you are connecting in a way that allows you to form true, meaningful connections."

Though most teachers disagree on the ideal way to describe rapport, they all agree that it is necessary for students and teachers to give it their all and to avoid burnout.

Most teachers would undoubtedly agree that each of the below is an excellent method to establish rapport.

- Smile as you greet students at the door.
- As rapidly as possible, learn the names of the students.
- Create classroom norms with the assistance of your pupils.
- Pose inquiries that will help you create rapport.
- Share a personal story with your students.
- Participate in school events or sponsor a club.
- At lunchtime, allow students to use your classroom.
- Celebrate your pupils' accomplishments and individuality.

But how can you do all of this when you're asked to teach online? It is undeniably more difficult than seeing your students face to face.

Because there aren't as many opportunities to develop relationships in an online setting as there are in a regular classroom, it's crucial to establish these places. To help you establish your classroom community, here is a list of simple online teaching best practices:

1. Greet your students at the online door with a smiling profile picture

Replace your internet profile picture with one of you smiling (if you haven't already).

This also entails logging into your class at least five to ten minutes before the start of each lesson and enthusiastically greeting each student as they log in.

Consider beginning each lesson with some form of happy, positive, and inviting rhetoric... perhaps even using the same expressions before each class.

But it is also important to be creative and always look for new ways to engage your students. This is important, in this period of online teaching, to go way beyond a smile and familiar greeting.

One experienced online educator shared her views on the topic with a researcher: "For those of us called upon to teach online in the fall, we will need to keep in mind that for the first time in history, if only because we are now too viewed daily on television, computer, and cell phone screens not only by our students but also by their parents and siblings, we will now all be judged by a higher standard . . . the standard of professional newscasters, weather reporters, and/or sports reporters. We, therefore, have to do more, come across better, in terms of our presentation, appearance, and demeanour. Like it or not, that's a new reality." (Paccone).

Use these links to help with your understanding and appreciation of the power of your profile picture:

- <u>Google Classroom: Change Your Profile Picture</u> (Teacher Tech with Alice Keeler, March 2020

- <u>Power of the 'Profile Pic' in Online Learning</u> <u>(Online Learning Insights,</u> June 2020)

- <u>The Research & Science Behind Finding Your Best Profile Picture</u> Buffer Library, March 2020)

2. Learn the names of your online students quickly

To do this, one instructor recommends begin the year by having each student speak her or his name as she or he enters his online classroom, if only so that he can hear and repeat it, allowing him to link the name to the face and voice more quickly. This teacher just believes that by doing so, he or she will be able to create rapport more effectively and quickly.

For those of us who struggle to remember students names here are two useful resources that will help your solve this problem:

- <u>Tips for Learning Students' Names</u> (Carnegie Mellon University Eberly Center, June 2020)
- <u>How to Remember Students' Names</u> (Edutopia, August 2014)

3. Use Flipgrid for engaging conversations

You and your students can use Flipgrid to respond to themes you've posted by making a selfie video. Students can view everyone's comments before responding with a video. Seeing and hearing you and their peers helps to establish a communal bond, even though they aren't simultaneous chats.

4. Make use of free time for a certain goal

Allowing students to join early 10 minutes before a live session to interact with you and each other is a terrific method to create essential, informal connections. Once a week, if possible, have a half-hour recess where students can log into a live conference room and just hang out.

You can facilitate subjects with amusing ice-breakers and "would you rather" inquiries if the conversation lags or lacks direction.

One art teacher has her junior art students tell jokes or talk about their day. These kinds of interactions are always pleasant, and her students enjoy every moment.

5. Have a show-and-tell session regularly

Most successful online teachers agree that rapport building online will prove more challenging than anticipated and as such, teachers should, increasingly share personal stories with their students.

They can also make use of show and tell in the virtual classroom! You choose the subject (their pet, their favourite clothing, a memorable vacation), and students use their video cameras and microphones to participate in a class. You may also put your show and tell at the bottom of a weekly email update. Students can contribute films or just photos with a caption, whichever is most convenient for them.

If you do decide to disclose your personal information, you'll need to consider what you want to share, when you want to share it, how much of it should be related to the content and/or skills you teach, and, probably most significantly, how you want to communicate it. Is it going to be via Zoom or Google Meet, Flipgrid, Twitter, Facebook, a blog post, or another method?

6. Make use of a class bulletin board

Padlet and *Google Docs* are excellent tools for building a collaborative message board in the classroom. Students can send one other birthday greetings, highlight significant events in their lives, and offer shoutouts and encouragements. Padlet's settings can be changed such that all messages must be authorized by you before being posted.

These kinds of initiatives are vital since students are away from the human contact that is a vital part of their socialization development. Using these apps will help students feel part of a classroom community, especially if the teacher ensures all students can contribute.

7. Never underestimate the power of a personal phone call

Reaching out and conversing with your students one-on-one is enough to establish a crucial bond. If you have a large class, make it a goal to speak with a particular number of students each week to ensure you're getting to everyone. Create a free *Google Voice* account if you don't have a business phone so your family doesn't have access to your personal number.

This is so important because students are going thru so much and sometimes it is not visible on screen but one phone call can help you understand why an assignment was late or poorly done. Reach out to your students, they need it!

8. Collaborate with your students to digitally create community norms

I propose Padlet or Google Docs for creating community rules in a digital classroom. They can be used as a forum for students to exchange their thoughts on norms and reach an agreement. Students will feel more a part of a classroom community if this is a shared endeavour, especially if the teacher guarantees that all students may contribute.

While meeting the challenges of a digital classroom, classroom norms should reflect universal classroom standards. For example, the concept of "one-mic, one-voice" can be expanded to incorporate the ability to mute oneself on Zoom when not speaking.

Every class session, these norms should be reviewed so that they become second nature. Students can reflect on their weekly commitment and rate their performance using an exit ticket tool such as a Google Forms survey or a SurveyMonkey poll. Giving students this kind of agency in setting standards fosters a culture of collaboration and agency.

It's crucial to remember that in these extraordinary times, rules must be adaptable to deal with unforeseen circumstances. The classroom environment should continue to be shaped by students. One teaching method used by successful online educators is the "Parking Lot," where students can write down and post any ideas or comments to be addressed as a class at a later time, while we can't duplicate the physical parking lot, Padlet allows teachers to provide a venue for kids to discuss their ideas on a shared page. Here are some links you will find useful:

- <u>Creating a Classroom Parking Lot</u> (Belolan, September 2013)

- <u>How to Collaborate Using Google Docs</u> (Zapier, March 2019)

- <u>Padlet as a Collaboration Tool</u> (Padlet, 2020)

- <u>Setting Community Agreement Activities</u> National School Reform Faculty, Spring 2014)

9. Ask Rapport Building Questions

Formulate questions to ask students at the start of class and at the end of class. You can have your students answer these questions in a *Google Form, Flipgrid* or while appearing on camera live. This kind of rapport allows you to learn valuable information about each of your students. You will also learn much of value from these three articles:

- <u>20 Questions to Get Kids Talking & Build Community</u> (Differentiated Teaching, 2020)

- <u>The Best Questions to use of Class Closing Activities</u> (Larry Ferlazzo, September 2013)

- <u>21 Social Distance-Friendly and Virtual Icebreakers Students Will Actually Have Fun With</u> (Bored Teachers, 2020)

Here is a sample of questions used by one educator in her online classes to build community rapport:

- Rank your interest in taking this class on a scale of 1–10

- Rank your speaking skills on a scale of 1–10

- Rank your writing skills on a Scale of 1–10

- What's your favorite subject?

- Describe your profile picture?

- <u>Would you rather </u>be the first person to explore a planet or be the inventor of a drug that cures a deadly disease?

- <u>Would you rather </u>lose the ability to read or lose the ability to speak?

- <u>Would you rather </u>always be 10 minutes late or always be 20 minutes early?

- Would you rather spend the rest of your life with a sailboat as your home or an RV as your home?

- Would you rather be an average person in the present or a king of a large country 2500 years ago?

- Would you rather be forced to dance every time you heard music or be forced to sing along to any song you heard? (Paccone)

10. Celebrate Your Students' Successes Online

One fantastic way to achieve this is to create a Facebook Group that can be viewed by anybody but can only be joined by your students. Some of the pieces you showcase could feature a performance, something baked, sketched, or written is also acceptable. Perhaps a piece of art or a speech. Any school-related work could be included in this category.

Another wonderful option to recognize your students' achievements online is to conduct interviews with them and then upload the results as a YouTube video or a podcast.

Below, two good examples.

• https://youtu.be/bOJ8MwNnsLw: Roberto Teekah, a final student from the E. R. Burrowes School of Art discusses his assignment on Colour Schemes and Theories, September 2021.

• The Craig McLaren Swan Titan Talk Interview: Craig is a San Marino High School junior and in this podcast, he tells us about his plans for rebuilding a used Mazda Miata, purchased shortly after the school shut down on March 13.

Rapport building can be a tricky thing to understand at times, here is an article that helps simplify the process: *Rapport-Building: Creating Positive Emotional Contexts for Enhancing Teaching and Learning*.

CHAPTER NINE:

Challenges to Online Teaching

"There can be infinite uses of the computer and of new technology [in training], but if the instructors themselves are not able to bring it to the learners and make it work, then it fails."
- U.S. Senator Nancy Kassebaum

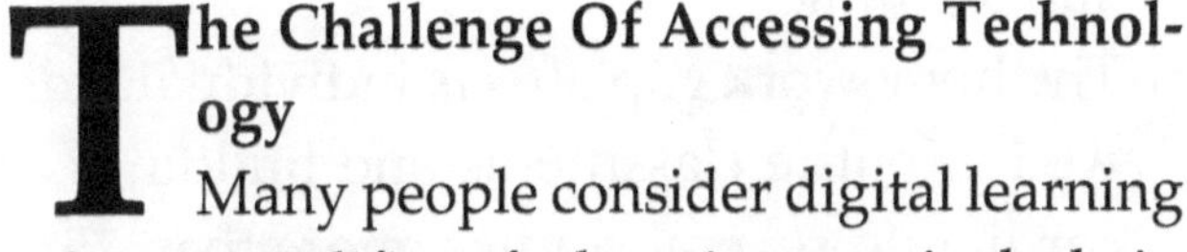

The Challenge Of Accessing Technology

Many people consider digital learning to be an amplifier of education, particularly in our increasingly mobile society. With this technology, great teachers may guide pupils to cognitive improvements and enhanced self-efficacy. Unfortunately, poor instruction is exacerbated. Technology, in the hands of inexperienced teachers, has the potential to reduce student performance.

Changes in teaching and learning are enabled by the promise of 1-to-1 and bring your own device (BYOD) methodologies. However, in far too many cases, teachers employ these new technologies to supplement traditional teaching methods: PDFs have taken the place of textbooks, applications have taken the place of worksheets, PowerPoint presentations have taken the place of poster boards, and the Internet has taken the place of library searches. The classroom structure, on the other hand, remains the same. Student outcomes do not improve unless teaching and learning are changed, as opposed to implementations that use actual student-centred strategies and technology to modify teaching and learning.

The homework gap affects individual kids as well as entire classrooms and buildings. According to several studies, more than 75% of teachers offer homework that necessitates the use of the Internet. This is a disadvantage to students who do not have home access and places pressure on teachers to find a solution for those students to accomplish homework without using the Internet.

This has two effects: The extra time and resources required to support two homework processes are costly; and if one student does not have technology at home, teachers are unable to transition their instruction to new pedagogies that rely on connectivity in the home to increase student accomplishment.

Finally, there is an unfairness that goes beyond the homework gap that is rarely discussed as part of the national connection debate in various countries. Students should be able to learn "anytime, anyplace," according to the 2010 National Educational Technology Plan of the United States of America. There is now a "mobility gap" between students who have 24/7 access to cellular broadband and those who do not. In developing and underdeveloped countries the problem is worst.

Having even one student who does not have home broadband access contributes to the homework gap. When students are unable to rely on appropriate Internet access, they must maintain old work habits and processes in addition to new, digitally-based processes. Of course, not all coursework will be digital, but for those that are, a lack of access is expensive.

Online Teaching Errors by Inexperienced teachers

When transferring to an online setting, even the most experienced teachers make a few frequent blunders. When you first begin teaching online, keep the following strategies in mind:

1. Failure to establish clear limits with pupils and parents

It can be difficult to unplug from your work when you work from home. It's even more difficult when students and families contact you at all hours of the night. It's tempting to pick up the phone or respond quickly but avoid it.

Share your availability hours with your family and stick to them. Simulate a typical school day, such as 7:30 a.m. to 3:30 p.m. Monday through Friday. It's critical that you take time to unplug, and everything your student requires may wait until the morning. Burnout among teachers is a significant problem.

2. Not putting new tools through their paces before introducing them to your students

Technology is wonderful when it works, as we all know. Something is bound to go wrong at some point. But that's fine! If something goes wrong, teachers adapt and move on, just like in the traditional classroom. Because trying out new technology for the first time can be scary, we recommend creating a mock class and employing some willing colleagues or family members as guinea pigs before implementing it with students.

3. Putting out too much information too quickly

Don't give your students difficult tasks or assignments without first teaching them how to use the technology. If you prepare families and students for this level of complexity, they will be able to handle it at some point. You don't want your pupil to spend more time attempting to figure out the instructions than really learning the material.

When assigning a learning objective that requires the use of a new digital tool, keep in mind that it may take your families an extra 30 minutes to an hour to become used to it. Provide detailed instructions as well as typical troubleshooting techniques. Better, assign a basic "mock assignment" before actually assigning a lesson. If it's a discussion board, for example, have students' first posting be about their family pet or what they did for fun over the weekend.

4. Maintaining Assessment Integrity

Academic integrity is a problem in both traditional and online learning settings. Some of the issues that people are concerned about include, but are not limited to:

Plagiarism happens when a student, whether

intentionally or unintentionally, presents another person's work as his or her own (i.e. copying parts of or whole papers off the Internet).

When a student gives his or her work to another individual to submit as their own, this is known as collusion. When a student fabricates information on a reference list, it is known as fabrication.

As instructors, we are faced with the task of identifying or developing effective techniques for preventing academic dishonesty and informing our students about the repercussions of betraying their academic integrity. Faculty must set clear policies, properly employ technology, and act ethically. It is vital to have a clear policy statement in your syllabus. It should not only define academic dishonesty for your students but also warn them about the repercussions. Finally, there are a few things to keep in mind when teaching online.

We've gone over a lot of different online teaching tactics and concepts. To sum up, here are three crucial insights to implement in your virtual classroom:

1. Maintain open lines of communication:
Communicate your expectations for behaviour early and regularly. Using various technologies such as emails, Remind 101, phone calls, and class message boards, keep lines of communication open. Weekly newsletters are an excellent method to foster a sense of community among families.

2. Adapt your classroom regularly:
Take the lessons you've already prepared and adapt them to the online setting using various Edtech tools. There's no need to recreate the wheel when there are so many excellent resources currently available. Albert provides an extensive collection of standards-aligned lessons and activities for students of all ages and subjects.

3. Engage students with a variety of asynchronous and synchronous activities:
Use a mix of asynchronous and synchronous activities to keep students engaged and satisfy diverse learner requirements. To develop strong student relationships, include intentional community-building activities like Show and Tell and time for free discussion.

Use the information where possible but re-member that one of the most powerful re-sources available to educators is each other!

The Disadvantages of Online Education
Technology availability:
In some cases, students and teachers may have restricted access to reliable or acceptable technology regularly. Several individuals may share a computer or mobile device in a single household, or they may rely on com-puters on campus or in public places (e.g. public library, Internet cafe, etc). Students and teachers may also have limited access to necessary software.

Use of the Internet:
Not all students and teachers have consistent or dependable internet connectivity. In many cases, internet access is limited to dial-up speed, or there is a monthly usage limit on their internet, limiting their capacity to access or engage with content.

Utilization of technology:
Certain technology and tools necessitate training. Technical training may not be read-ily available to students or teachers in some cases.

Separation:

It can be a lonely and isolated experience for teachers who do not have peer support for their online projects.

Information overload:

In many cases, the amount of information, "how-to" instructions, help, and resources available online can become overwhelming and confusing if not effectively managed. It can be challenging for students and teachers to determine which are relevant or vital.

Some of the challenges to online teaching is directly linked to equity in schools, district and countries.

Randy Bentinck

CHAPTER TEN:

The Question of Digital Equity

*"A lack of digital access is a lack of access to education period," - **Terry Godwaldt***

Most students now have access to the Internet while at school, thanks to programs implemented by some countries, which provides subsidized Internet connection and financing to schools and districts.

However, after students get home, they may not have access to high-speed Internet or a device other than a smartphone, leading to the so-called homework gap, as defined by policymakers. According to a Pew Research Center (The Pew Research Center is a nonpartisan American think tank based in Washington, D.C. It provides information on social issues, public opinion, and demographic trends shaping the United States and the world) survey, 35% of families with school-aged children and a yearly income of less than $35,000 do not have access to high-speed Internet.

Furthermore, according to the National Center for Education Statistics, only 61 percent of school-aged children had Internet access at home in 2015, even though 80 percent of eighth-grade students said they needed a computer to complete homework. While the consequences of the Digital Divide have been mitigated to some extent for children while in school, according to the Consortium of School Networking's (CoSN) most current infrastructure assessment, fewer than 10% of district officials believe that ALL of their students have access outside of school (Strategies For Teachers Tackling Digital Equity In The Classroom).

What Exactly Is Digital Equity?

First and foremost, the phrase must be defined. Digital equality refers to all students and teachers having equal access to and capacity to use technology. You may hear the terms digital equity and digital inclusion used interchangeably. Digital inclusion refers to the methods we use to achieve digital equity.

It is easier to describe digital equity than it is to solve it. It is about ensuring that students have equal access to technology such as gadgets, software, and the internet, as well as skilled instructors to assist them in navigating those tools. When you consider all of the students on the 'educational playfield' – those from low-income districts or rural communities, children with physical or learning disabilities, and girls or minority students who do not have the same opportunities and support to prepare them for careers in technology – that can be a tall order.

The mandatory COVID-19 shutdowns quickly changed the definition of "school." Schools, which were no longer a physical, community environment for learning, moved their emphasis from learning experiences and classroom administration to a new set of priorities. Teachers must learn new technology, assist students' well-being, manage varied home circumstances, and promote learning via a device while also supporting their own families. Concerns about teacher training, screen time, and the efficacy of technology vanished overnight as schools immediately embraced technology to facilitate learning. This quick transformation also compelled schools to tackle students' unequal origins, exposing the living reality for many children

who do not have a safe or quiet learning environment.

The digital gap exists

Many students, particularly those from black and brown communities, underdeveloped and developing countries have dispropor-tionately low access to basic internet, which is required for online learning. Despite schools dipping deep into their resources to purchase devices and Wi-Fi hotspots for children in need, disparities continue. Millions of chil-dren would be unable to "study from home" if this did not exist.

Digital equity entails more than just having access to devices and the internet. Remote learning necessitates the use of digital prod-ucts produced by technology companies who sell their products to schools by teachers and students. Even when all children have equal access to the internet, schools must guarantee that technology companies take into account how racial bias still affects children today. The same standards that schools use to inves-tigate instructor bias and require culturally relevant curriculum should also be used to evaluate the software that schools utilize. The COVID-19 dilemma provides an opportunity for schools to restructure students' learning experiences – to look critically about how, or rather, for whom, our education system is constructed. We must accept responsibility for how our system disadvantages these students by ensuring that schools promote students' needs and EdTech firms commit to racial equity in the same manner that they commit to data privacy and accessibility.

Many localities do not provide all pupils with basic access to technology. Before the COVID shutdown, around 17% of US teenagers were unable to do homework due to a lack of access. Additional, 12% had to rely on public Wi-Fi for the purpose, which grew increasingly challenging when public access points were offline for months at a time.

Simultaneously, access to technology is more vital than ever. Even before COVID, technology was essential for college students and most jobs. Gone are the days when office workers had to learn to use computers but other professions could get away with it. Even blue-collar workers are expected to comprehend technology to some extent these days.

As the world acclimated to the pandemic, digital access became a lifeline for families all around the country and the world. But what happened to the 17 percent who didn't have access, as well as the 12 percent whose public Wi-Fi alternatives had run out? If we do not bridge the digital barrier, these students will be unable to access their education remotely, let alone be prepared for college or the workplace. In a nutshell, we will have let them down.

Several Impediments to Digital Equity

On the surface, it appears that giving each student a digital gadget will address the problem, but the solution is rarely so simple. Various things must be considered.

The Cost Of Services And Devices

The first and most obvious issue is the current cost of technology. Devices start in hundreds of dollars and can cost thousands of dollars if sophisticated capabilities are added. When you factor in the cost of home internet or mobile data, you have an expense that many families cannot afford.

Inadequate Internet Access

It would be a mistake to believe that all financially successful households have equal access. The issue isn't always related to money in the family. Internet connectivity in rural locations may be limited by availability rather than cost. If some of your students live outside of town, they may be able to afford a dozen horses and a crew to care for them while having slow internet or no home Wi-Fi at all.

Parental Comprehension

Finally, even if your students can buy technology and have access to high-speed internet, they may encounter parental understanding issues. Parents who did not grow up with technology may be unable to assist students if they do not understand how to use technology themselves. This is especially true for pupils raised by grandparents or whose parents are older, as well as those who have immigrated from developing nations. Others, on the other hand, may have simply never learned about technology because they were uninterested in it or did not believe they needed it.

Providing Devices Is Insufficient

So, how do schools assist their students in bridging the big technological divide? What else should be done if giving each student a Chromebook isn't enough?

First and foremost, students require internet connectivity. This means lower-income families will be able to afford an internet connection, and those living in more remote places will have access to high-speed hotspots.

Following that, schools must invest in the community beyond the students in their care. Parents must be taught how to use electronic devices. They must also be educated about the perils of unregulated internet access for children's thinking. Free community workshops and evening programs can help to overcome this barrier.

Finally, students require more than just access; they must also be safe online. This means that devices offered to students must be restricted so that children do not gain access to hazardous materials. Products such as GoGuardian AdminTM can aid in the monitoring and management of devices in K-12 schools. Students can be protected from internet fraud and adult materials by using a comprehensive web filter.

Methods by Which People Are Attempting to Bridge the Gap

The situation may appear overwhelming to teachers and school administrators struggling with budgetary constraints and pandemic measures. However, some individuals are making significant progress toward digital equity in a variety of ways.

In the United States of America, for example, several states have been implementing digital equity plans. The Digital Equity Strategic Plan for 2019-2024 in San Francisco will have a significant impact on the community. Its objectives include providing affordable internet to the entire city, increasing digital literacy among all people, and providing long-term advantages to the community as a whole.

The Digital Equity Initiative of Washington State is intended to provide tools for remote learning across the entire state. The program is seeking donations from individual and corporate donors to give kids with devices, broadband connectivity, and technical help.

The North Carolina Department of Information Technology has been hard at work, striving for statewide broadband connectivity. Even before the pandemic, the department was putting in the groundwork to make this dream a reality.

Boston is aiming to deliver affordable and reliable internet to public spaces throughout the city. Its Digital Equity Fund is building fibre-optic networks while also offering free WiFi. It provides digital skills training and assists in making digital technologies available to the community.

Finally, Common Sense Media has a plan to assist states and school districts in promoting digital fairness through evidence-based K-12 solutions. The organization is seeking to persuade Congress to invest in the infrastructure that will enable digital equity across the country.

Whatever the challenges in your community, there are steps you can do to bridge the digital divide. Other countries around the globe can learn from these initiatives by examining them and learn from the steps they are taking. Then, collaborate with local authorities to promote digital equity in their schools.

CHAPTER ELEVEN:

Digital Tools for Teachers and Students

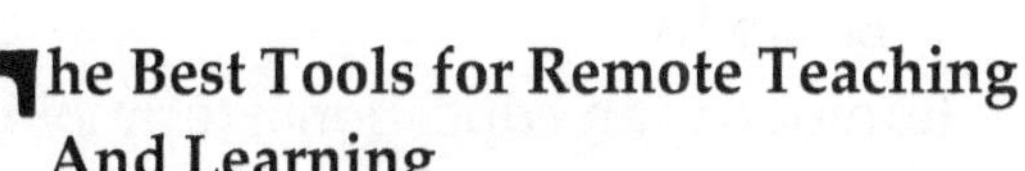

The Best Tools for Remote Teaching And Learning

Technology plays a critical part in the processes of teaching children and adolescents in the new era of learning. The abrupt switch to remote education has presented many teachers and students with a variety of obstacles, ranging from a lack of internet connection to locating the appropriate tools to overcome the constraints of online education. We've gathered a list of tools that you may use to improve your experience teaching online, or remote teaching as it's more commonly known these days.

You can browse the list and choose the best

online teaching tools for your remote teaching needs.

The Top Digital Education Tools for Teachers and Students

Hundreds of digital education technologies have been developed to offer students' autonomy, enhancing academic process administration, increasing collaboration, and facilitating communication between professors and students. Here are 11 of the most popular.

1. Edmodo

Edmodo is an educational technology that integrates a social network and connects professors and students. Teachers can use this one too, among other things, build online collaborative groups, administrate and supply instructional materials, monitor student performance, and interact with parents. Edmodo has over 34 million users who collaborate to make learning more enriching, individualized and aligned with the opportunities provided by technology and the digital world.

2. Socrative

Socrative is a system designed by a group of entrepreneurs and engineers that are passionate about education. It allows professors to build exercises or educational games that students may complete using mobile devices such as smartphones, laptops, or tablets. Teachers may monitor the outcomes of the exercises and, based on them, adapt following sessions to make them more personalized.

3. Projeqt

Projeqt is a tool for creating multimedia presentations with dynamic slides that include interactive maps, connections, online quizzes, Twitter timelines, and videos, among other features. During a class session, teachers can share academic presentations with students that have been graphically converted to different devices.

During a class session, teachers can share academic presentations with students that have been graphically converted to different devices.

4. Thinglink

Thinglink enables instructors to create interactive graphics that incorporate music, noises, words, and photographs. These can be posted on other websites or social media platforms like Twitter and Facebook. Thinglink allows teachers to design learning techniques that arouse students' curiosity through inter-active information that can broaden their knowledge.

5. TED-Ed

This website enables for the democratization of information access for both teachers and students. People can actively participate in the learning process of others here.

6. cK-12

cK-12 is a website dedicated to lowering the price of academic publications for the K12 market in the United States and around the world. To accomplish this goal, this platform provides an open-source interface that ena-bles for the creation and distribution of in-structional content via the internet, which can be updated and includes films, audios, and interactive exercises. It can also be printed and meet the editorial standards in each re-gion. The books developed in cK-12 can be customized to meet the needs of every in-structor or student.

7. ClassDojo

ClassDojo is a technique for improving stu-dent behaviour in which professors provide quick feedback to their students so that good behaviour in class is rewarded with points and students have a more open attitude toward the learning process. For working collaboratively, ClassDojo sends students real-time notifications such as 'Well Done David!' and '+1.' The information gathered on student behaviour can later be shared with parents and officials over the internet.

8. eduClipper

Teachers and students can use this platform to share and discover references and educational materials. In eduClipper, you may collect information found on the internet and then share it with members of previously created groups, allowing you to manage academic content found online more effectively, improve research methodologies, and keep a digital record of what students accomplished during the course. Similarly, it allows teachers to organize a virtual class with their pupils and establish a portfolio where all of their work is saved.

9. Storybird

Storybird attempts to improve pupils' writing and reading skills through storytelling. Teachers can use this application to produce interactive and artistic books online using a simple and easy-to-use interface. The tales that are made can be incorporated on blogs, emailed, and printed, among other things. Teachers can also use Storybird to collaborate on projects with their students, provide constant feedback, and manage lessons and grades.

10. Animoto

Animoto is a digital tool that allows you to quickly and easily produce high-quality films from any mobile device, exciting pupils and helping to improve academic teaching. The Animoto interface is user-friendly and practical, allowing teachers to generate audiovisual content that is tailored to the needs of their students.

11. Kahoot!

Kahoot! is a question-and-answer-based educational platform. Teachers can use this tool to generate quizzes, conversations, and surveys to supplement academic teaching. The information is shown in the classroom, and students answer questions while playing and learning. Kahoot! encourages game-based learning, which boosts student engagement and fosters a dynamic, sociable, and enjoyable learning environment.

13. Hypothes.is

Use Hypothesis to hold discussions, read socially, organize your research, and take personal notes for reflective teaching, for example.

14. Factile

What is Factile? The game-based learning platform is a free learning platform that lets teachers create engaging jeopardy-style quiz games for the remote or in-person classroom.

15. Buncee

Buncee is a creation and presentation tool for students and educators to create interactive classroom content, allowing learners of all ages to visualize concepts and communicate creatively.

16. Wakelet

Save, organize and present multimedia content with your students, teachers and learning communities with Wakelet (which is a free tool for teachers).

17. Flipgrid

Flipgrid a free, simple way to foster short

video-based discussions on classroom topics. See Ways To Use Flipgrid In The Classroom.

18. Parlay

This tool helps you create a custom discussion prompt just for your class. Each student reviews the materials provided and submits a unique response to the discussion prompt.

19. Seesaw

This popular tool (also useful in the physical classroom) empower students to independently document their learning. See how one teacher uses Seesaw in her classroom.)

20. Microsoft Whiteboard

Bring your virtual, remote teaching classroom together on the same virtual canvas, around the world and across devices. Brainstorm simultaneously in the Whiteboard app or from your browser window.

21. IXL

K-2 online learning for students. This won't help you plan lessons directly but students can practice skills, take quick diagnostic assessments, and see their progress over time.

22. CK-12

CK-12 allows you to 'create' digital textbooks

and lessons from materials and resources in science and math through their library of free online textbooks, videos, exercises, flash-cards, and real-world applications for over 5000 concepts across the content areas.

23. Diigo

According to Wikipedia, Diigo is "a social bookmarking website that allows signed-up users to bookmark and tag Web pages. Additionally, it allows users to highlight any part of a webpage and attach sticky notes to specific highlights or to a whole page."

24. Alchem.ie

Resources, tools, and tips to teach and learn K-12 Chemistry online.

25. Nearpod

Software to create lessons with informative and interactive assessment activities.

26. Google Classroom (or Google Drive)

Microsoft OneDrive is a good alternative to Google Drive and useful here as well.

27. Slack

Trello and Redbooth are good alternatives to Slack as well, depending on your usage case/needs.

28. Netboard.me

Collect, organize and share any web content. Create Web pages with texts, links, documents, videos, photos, presentations, etc.

29. Prezi

With a basic subscription and a profile that states you're an education professional, you get PreziNext and PreziVideo for free. You can also access designer templates, millions of reusable presentations, etc.

30. Slidesmania

Free PowerPoint templates or Google Slides themes for education. You can find simple, formal and even fun templates.

31. Sutori

Organize, plan, and center instruction. The collaborative nature and ease of use makes Sutori the perfect companion for student and teacher presentations.

32. Symbaloo

Symbaloo is a cloud-based application that allows users to organize and categorize web links in the form of buttons, offering its PRO version to all educators at no cost.

31. Zoom

Google Meet, Hangouts, and other alternatives to Zoom are available as well. Further, you can extend its functionality for schools with 20 Of The Best Zoom Tools For Teachers.

32. EdPuzzle

Video lesson creation software with lots of usable content.

33. Kahoot

A well-known tool across education, Kahoot is a game-based learning platform that seeks to bring engagement and fun to students at school or at home.

34. Loom

Loom makes it very simple to easily record and share video: capture your screen, record your front-facing camera, and narrate it all at once, then instantly share with students with a link.

35. Screencastify

Screencastify is the safest, simplest video creation tool for teachers and students.
Teachers in 70% of US school districts use Screencastify to improve student learning. It helps make learning more personal in your

blended, hybrid or flipped classroom with on-demand videos.

36. Pear Deck
Facilitates the design of engaging instructional content with various integration features.

37. Squigl
Content creation platform that transforms speech or text into animated videos.

39. Google App Hub for Distance Learning
This is a collection of Google for Education Technology Partner Apps.

40. Thinglink
Tools to create interactive images, videos, and other multimedia resources.

CHAPTER TWELVE:

Free Online Professional Development

*"Technology will never replace great teachers, but in the hands of great teachers, it's transformational." – **George Couros***

Not every teacher or educator might work in a system or a country where they have the much-needed support to transition to online teaching smoothly or continue to upgrade themselves. Here is a list of resources to aid your professional development and licensure requirements.

If you're looking for a free, online approach to achieve your professional development goals or criteria, you've got a lot of possibilities. The compiled list below offers a wide variety for you to consider, along with a brief description and the requirements for finishing each one. Please ensure to double-check that any solutions you choose fit the specific licensure criteria of your state or district before proceeding.

TeachThought PD

In-Person PD, online workshops, and blended professional development support.

They design and deliver professional learning that:

- is relevant to your context

- helps you plan and improve instruction

- is driven by your questions

- includes hands-on strategies

- is highly interactive

- is sustained over time

TeachThought University

Modern professional development in the cloud. Solving the problem of access and innovation in modern professional development for teachers.

Zoom Video Tutorials

A wide range of video tutorial to help your master this resource. They are hard at work to provide you with the best 24x7 global support experience as part of this ongoing commitment.

Seesaw Training and Professional Development

They provide training for teachers to help them learn the ins and outs of Seesaw. You can join them live or watch a recording at your own pace.

How To Use FlipGrid: A Guide For Teachers

Flipgrid is a free, education-focused platform to create and share short videos. This link provides a visual guide for teachers on how to use flipgrid.

Remote Teaching Tips

Resources and tips for remote education during school closures.

PBS TeacherLine

PBS TeacherLine offers 15, 30, and 45-hour courses that are normally acceptable for continuing education credits. Through university collaborations, you can even receive graduate-level credit. Each course is self-paced and may be finished in your own time.

Coursera

Coursera is a learning platform that collaborates with colleges all around the world to provide free and open courses. There are many professional development courses available for teachers, including:

- Supporting Children with Difficulties in Reading and Writing

- Teaching Character and Creating Positive Classrooms

- Motivating Gen Z Learners: What Parents and Teachers Need to Know

TeachingTolerance

Check out TeachingTolerance if you're seeking professional development that focuses on social-emotional learning. Their professional development section contains a plethora of webinars and self-paced learning activities on themes such as diversity, leadership, and empathy in the classroom.

LearnersEdge

LearnersEdge provides free on-demand webinar recordings on a wide range of topics, including mindfulness and mental health awareness, as well as reading and writing. After completing the webinar, you will be able to obtain a certificate to meet your individual professional development needs.

Canvas

Canvas provides a variety of online, self-paced professional development opportunities for instructors, many of which are free. Here are some sample courses to give you an idea of what this resource has to offer:

- The Art and Craft of Remote Teaching

- Safe & Resilient Schools: Mental Health

- Supporting Girls in STEAM

Learning for Justice

Learning for Justice maintains a library of on-demand webinars on promoting equity and access in schools. You can learn about topics such as How to Be an Ally in the Classroom and Responding to Hate and Bias at School here.

If your district allows webinars to be used to complete professional development needs, this can be an excellent choice.

SciLearn

Whether you're a STEM teacher or just interested in learning more about the scientific side of education, SciLearn delivers webinars on the neuroscience of learning. Among the most recent sessions are:

- How to Rewire the Brains of Struggling Learners

- Engaging All Students with Poverty in Mind

- Developing Executive Function from Kindergarten Through High School

National Education Association

For instructors seeking professional development credits, the National Educators Association (NEA) hosts live webinars and maintains a website with recorded webinars. The group also hosts a podcast called School Me, which, though not credit-worthy, provides a wealth of bite-sized "life tips" for educators.

Sanford Inspire

Webinars are a quick and simple method to accomplish professional development hours online, but if you prefer a more hands-on approach, try taking one of Sanford Aspire's free professional development courses. After completing the course and passing the assessment, you will receive a professional development certificate that you can submit to your district and potentially redeem for credit.

Association for Supervision and Curriculum Development

The Association for Supervision and Curriculum Development (ASCD) is a professional organization that promotes the development of teachers and educators.

The website of the Association for Supervision and Curriculum Development (ASCD) contains a vast archive of webinars for instructors and live webinar alternatives for ASCD members. Each session, like the others on this list, can be redeemed for an hour of credit, provided it fits the precise conditions for your license renewal.

SimpleK12

SimpleK12's slogan is "professional development in your pajamas," and they provide educational webinars that may be seen at home. Although some webinars are restricted to site members only, many others are open to the public.

The Library of Congress

The Library of Congress provides professional development programs that you can create yourself, such as Understanding Copyright and Primary Sources and Inquiry. These are intended for educators who want to offer their professional development course to their colleagues, which you can then submit to your district for licensure credit.

Some online webinars and courses can count toward one hour of professional development.

Institute for Arts Integration and STEAM

The arts and humanities are essential for instilling in youngsters creativity and critical thinking. You can get free toolkits and audio training on bringing arts into the classroom through the Institute for Arts Integration and STEAM, several of which can be redeemed for professional development hours.

edWeb

edWeb may easily fit into your schedule because it offers both live and on-demand webinars. Because of the variety of topics covered, the webinars can be excellent free professional development for both early elementary and secondary school teachers.

Facing History

Facing History offers both free and paid courses, webinars, and video professional development opportunities for combating racism in schools. If you are unable to attend a live event, there is an archive of on-demand webinars and seminars available.

SHAPE America

This resource is for you if you are a health or physical education teacher or if you simply want to learn more about health education. The Society of Health and Physical Educators' website, SHAPE America, offers a plethora of free webinars on K-12 health education. Here are a few examples:

- Ideas for Equitable and Accessible Teaching in Health and Physical Education

- No-Cost Digital Resources to Support Social, Emotional and Physical Wellness

- Trauma-Sensitive Practices in Health Education

TeachersFirst Workshops

Many of the alternatives on this list are self-guided or pre-recorded, however, Teachers-First may be more your speed if you like interactive professional development. These free, live workshops are 90 minutes long and are held after school hours for teachers who have a hectic workday.

ShareMyLesson

ShareMyLesson is a website that allows you to share your lessons with others.

ShareMyLesson provides a wide range of short professional development sessions for teachers, administrators, and parents that were recorded during their 2019 virtual conference. If these sessions match your specific license criteria, you can watch them on your own time and gain one hour of continuing education credit for each.

KQED Teach

You can take digital media courses through KQED Teach to help you get the most out of educational technology in your classroom. Whether you want to learn how to create a teacher blog, spot internet misinformation, or even try your hand at video production, there is a course for you.

EdWeek Special Education Webinars

EdWeek provides live and recorded webinars on professional development in education for special education teachers. After viewing a webinar, you will be able to obtain a certificate confirming one hour of professional development. The following are some recent webinar topics:

- Equity, Care and Connection: New SEL Tools and Practices to Support Students and Adults

- A Seat at the Table: Strategies & Tips for Complex Decision-Making

- Making Digital Literacy a Priority: An Administrator's Perspective

CHAPTER THIRTEEN:

Online Classes and Your Mental Health

"The greatest weapon against stress is our ability to choose one thought over another. "
– William James

Teachers' mental health is deteriorating in ways they have never seen before during the pandemic. The load is especially apparent for moms who are guiding both their pupils and their own children through online learning.

Because of the COVID-19 pandemic, schools and colleges around the world switched to online programs. During the epidemic, everyone's health and safety were of the utmost importance, and online education was the only viable choice.

It was first both comfy and convenient. For parents, no more driving their children to school, no more preparing snacks, and some children even attend school in their jammies. However, in the long run, students, parents, and even professors and teachers have recognized the difficulties of online education, particularly concerning one's mental health.

Students, parents, and even professors' mental health suffer as a result of online classes. Individuals with pre-existing mental health issues may experience worsening symptoms. Consider what it would be like for a child to spend hours every day in front of Zoom, with no social connection or recreation with their peers. Parents are increasingly acting as teachers and becoming more active in their children's homework. Teachers and academics are under pressure to give quality learning without face-to-face classes due to growing workloads.

In this chapter, we explore how online learning settings might affect the mental health of teachers, tutors, professors, students, and parents. We will also provide you with some pointers on how to deal with the difficulties of online learning.

Many educators who are exposed to their students' personal issues during online learning may be encountering conditions that have a negative influence on their mental health, academic progress, and school culture.

"Kids can act normally at school even if they are having issues at home," says Mandy Froehlich, an education consultant. "During this period, students may also be more vocal about suspected increases in drinking, drug use, or abuse at home. Meanwhile, teachers are aware that these youngsters no longer have a safe place to go seven hours a day, as they did before school closures."

Compassion fatigue, in which caregivers provide so much support that they do not have time to care for themselves, and vicarious trauma, in which carers experience the trauma-related symptoms that their pupils do, are two conditions that educators may experience.

"These conditions are not only detrimental to a teacher's personal life but they can, in the most basic sense, lead to teacher disengagement, such as failing to form relationships with students or contributing to a negative culture," says Froehlich, author of The Fire Within: Lessons from Failure That Have Ignited a Passion for Learning and Reignite the Flames: Finding Our Passion and Purpose for Learning. "It is critical for administration to understand why their teachers disengage so that they can assist educators in helping themselves."

Here are three steps that school administrators can take to assist staff in dealing with teacher compassion fatigue and vicarious trauma.

1. Make mental health resources available to teachers

Leaders must provide mental health services or bring in health professionals to reduce teacher stress and help educators comprehend what they are going through. "Failure to recognize the source of their problems could lead to instructors believing they are suffering from burnout or demoralization, for example, and thus seeking the wrong ways to receive help," Froehlich says.

2. Keep boundaries in place

Administrators must be mindful of faculty work-life balance. "If you're going to send an email at 6 p.m., for example, make sure your faculty understands that you don't expect a response at that time," Froehlich advises. "When I was a tech director, I would sometimes email late at night, not because I expected my employees to react right away, but because it was the only time I could get to my email. This is something that needs to be communicated."

Reducing teacher burden by ensuring that each step in new projects serves a purpose can also help. This can be accomplished by removing non-essential compliance-related activities. "Do not ask your teachers to give up their lives for their work," Froehlich advises. "They will try to do this on their own and will not require assistance."

3. Recognize the complexity of mental health insurance

Teachers suffering from compassion fatigue or vicarious trauma cannot seek care continually, so districts must understand how their insurance works so that faculty and staff can seek help promptly when needed. "To make my point, I often relate a true story of a period when I was going through a major depression and had to phone 14 or 15 different people on our insurance list just to get an appointment that was three months away," Froehlich adds. "Even if your insurance says a doctor's practice is accepting new patients, they aren't always. It is critical to understand the insurance being acquired, as well as their dedication to keeping their databases, updating their information, and supporting an easy mental health process."

Leaders should coordinate with community mental health specialists to plan visits to schools to work with teachers and children. "Teachers aren't going to take time out of their day to see a counselor until their condition becomes unbearable. Making services more comfortable and accessible is a more proactive strategy, according to Froehlich.

"Teachers must be the ones to say, 'Oh, I recognize this in myself, and I want to do better,'" she adds. The best thing administrators can do is provide teachers with the education and support they need to take the next step on their own."

4. Virtual Learning Can Cause Fatigue

During the COVID era, there was a newly developed word called "Zoom Fatigue." Zoom Fatigue refers to sensations of tiredness after participating in long Zoom classes or video conference calls. Although it is not an official diagnosis, Zoom fatigue does exist, particularly in virtual learning. There is information overload in an online class, and staring at a screen for lengthy periods is psychologically tiring. It is more difficult for kids to learn new knowledge, and even though they are only sitting in front of a computer, they feel physically exhausted. Virtual learning weariness is real, and it can cause anxiety and tension in students and teachers alike.

5. Lack of Interaction and Social Isolation

Schools are not just places where students learn new things from books; they are also places where friendships are formed and wonderful memories are made. Social contacts are the best way to learn communication and social skills. Kids, teens, and even instructors need to mingle and connect with their peers.

However, since the COVID pandemic, there has been a dearth of connection, and pupils are experiencing social isolation. This has a significant impact on a student's mental health. Loneliness, a lack of motivation, and isolation result from a lack of social engagement in online learning.

Even grownups, right? sense an empty hole when they don't see their buddies. In their formative years, young adults require social engagement. To learn how to socialize, children need to go on play dates with other children their age. Professors, too, require engagement with their colleagues. Nobody wants to feel alone and alone. This is one of the primary reasons why online learning can have an impact on mental health.

6. Increased Anxiety and Stress

During the school day, pupils in a standard classroom layout follow a normal schedule. When it's time to get up when it's time to go to school when it's time for class when it's time to complete homework when it's time for lunch, when it's time to engage with friends, and when it's time to participate in extracurricular activities. Online learning is never the same.

It's difficult to stay focused on online classes. Students were unable to concentrate in class due to the separation between home life and class time, the lack of a consistent schedule, and distractions at home. As a result, students procrastinate and put things off, and deadlines are missed. Both students and their parents experience pressure, worry, and anxiety as a result of this.

7. The Parent's Mental Health Get Affected Too

Online learning has an impact not only on students but also on their parents. Parents are now acting as proxy educators, tutors, and are becoming more active in their children's schooling to ensure that they learn effectively and maintain good grades. How can a parent tutor Physics if they aren't excellent at it?

What about work-from-home parents and dads who are overburdened with their jobs while also assisting their children with their online classes? It's draining, and it's producing a lot of stress.

8. Even the Teachers and Faculty Get Stressed Out Too

Have you seen popular social media photographs of tenured professors struggling to teach their pupils online? They have years of classroom experience, but teaching with electronic gadgets has not been their strongest suit. There is also the pressure and concern that instructors would lose their jobs as a result of school closures. There is also the added workload of ensuring that their kids receive a high-quality education. These are all producing concerns, and it has been difficult for teachers' mental health as well.

Online Learning Pros

Although online learning has the potential to negatively affect students' and parents' mental health, it also has advantages, notably in terms of family connection and relationships. Staying at home allows for more time for family bonding. Parents who were previously unable to spend much time with their children due to hectic work schedules can now devote more time to their children. This is very useful while trying to comprehend your adolescent. Some students who have been bullied at school may find online learning beneficial. They are more productive when they feel safe at home. They will be able to avoid the worry of being bullied at school. Although parents should be aware that bullying can take numerous forms, they should also be aware that cyberbullying exists.

How to Take Care of Your Mental Health

Because of the stress of online classes, there are numerous strategies to care for your mental health. This section includes suggestions for parents, students, and teachers. Here are some strategies to consider:

Have a Designated Work/Study Space: Choose a location at home with fewer interruptions so you can focus on work or school. You will be more concentrated and productive as a result. Choose a peaceful space, put up barriers, and make it a rule at home not to bother anyone during work or school hours. You can set a barrier this way and be less overwhelmed by distractions.

Encourage Healthy Behaviors: Encouraging healthy habits is one method to care for one's mental health. This includes eating well, getting enough sleep, getting adequate physical activity, and taking care of your physical health. You will notice an improvement in your mood, higher energy levels, and overall mental well-being if you practice healthy habits regularly.

Maintain a consistent schedule: Routine labour may be dull for some, but sticking to a routine adds order and organization to one's life. It allows you to complete the things you set out for the day and avoid cramming at the last minute. There will be days when you lose sight of time and delay activities that must be completed. Maintain a consistent routine by sleeping and waking up at the same time every day. Stick to work and school schedules, arrange breaks, and adhere to study time routines. As you incorporate organization into your daily routine, you will feel more productive and less stressed.

Encourage physical activity:
Since the advent of home learning, kids have had little opportunity to engage in physical activity. Unlike in the past, children can now run around the playground, climb four flights of stairs to their classroom, or ride their bikes from school to home. Encourage physical activities for children, such as riding, taking a walk in the park, or doing any physical activity in the backyard with the family. Any physical activity creates feel-good hormones in the body, which can aid in the improvement of a person's mental health. Furthermore, spending time outside prevents emotional and mental weariness.

Advice For Parents
Set a Positive Tone at Home: To reduce stress and worry, parents should set a positive tone

at home. This involves avoiding angry outbursts, speaking softly, and not putting too much strain on yourself or your children.

Take Breaks: Taking breaks from the day-to-day hustle and bustle is essential. Take a power nap, meditate, go outside for a while, and breathe deeply if you're bored of your child's education. Go for a short walk to clear your head. Do not push yourself to fulfill deadlines if it means alienating yourself from your loved ones. Set the books aside if it is not a school day and take time to enjoy the weekend. Have movie evenings with your kids, picnic in the lawn, or spend quality time outside. Because of all your hard work, you and your children deserve to have happy moments.

Finding Help for Your Mental Health

This COVID-19 pandemic has posed a significant challenge to all of us. Face-to-face lessons may not return anytime soon in some states, and all we can do is adapt to their challenges. Along with the above-mentioned techniques to care for your mental health, you should also consider obtaining treatment from a mental health expert.

Fortunately, you don't have to leave your house to see a therapist. The Kentucky Counseling Center's Telehealthcare Service is only a few mouse clicks away. Speak with a therapist right away to learn how to take care of your mental health during these tough times. Keep yourself safe and healthy!

Learn Self-Care: Prioritize self-care above all else. You devote your life as a parent to making your children happy and healthy. But don't forget to look after yourself as well. Do activities you like, pick up a new interest, catch up with friends, and indulge yourself. You must also be psychologically well to be there for your children.

CHAPTER FOURTEEN:

Conclusion

"Online learning is not the next big thing, it is the now big thing." - **Donna J. Abernathy**

———❦———

Karl M. Kapp, a Professor of Instructional Technology at Bloomsburg University stated,

Instructional designers need to run, not walk, away from classroom-based thinking and get to the point of providing short, quick business-focused learning points that are easily accessible when and where our learners need them. This means leveraging new technologies to deliver non-traditional instruction.

In a rapidly changing teaching-learning environment where technology continues to play a major role understanding and simplifying its use is vital to all educators and education stakeholders. In one research, 76% of teachers claim that technology enables them to respond to a variety of learning styles (Ribbonfish).

Online Teaching Simplified sought to provide

educators with tips not only to help them understand the technologies needed to deliver effective teaching and learning but also to make the right choices that would maximise and make the process of delivering educational goals and outcomes seamless with fewer stresses along the way.

The benefits of online teaching are many and both students and educators profit from it when it is executed effectively. With online teaching instructors have more flexibility while teaching since they can target different learning styles and employ different technologies.

Students who may not take part actively in traditional classroom settings may benefit from online classes, and instructors who teach online have access to a plethora of technology to make classes more fascinating. One prominent research found that 74% of teachers claim digital content in schools increases students' engagement (Ribbonfish).

Online professors, like online students, appreciate the flexibility and convenience of the medium. They can teach from the convenience of their own homes, and it does not require them to be at a specific location at a specific time to teach or connect with their students.

However, to maximize the benefits of the online environment, online teachers must remember that active learning is one of the keys to success in the online classroom. To ensure that their courses make the most of the online medium while applying new strategies and technologies. The practical tips and tools provided in this text provide you with many of those technologies to make your online teaching experience more rewarding for the teaching-learning process.

REFERENCES

1. "20 Free Online Professional Development Resources for Teachers." Waterford.org, 28 May 2021, www.waterford.org/resources/free-online-professional-developmment-for-teachers/.

2. "Why Is Online Teaching Important? - Introduction to Teaching Online." Google Sites, www.sites.google.com/a/hawaii.edu/new-de-faculty-orientation/Step-1.

3. 21 Strategies for Teaching Online: The Ultimate Guide. Albert Resources. (2020, November 24). https://www.albert.io/blog/strategies-for-teaching-online/.

4. Athuraliya, Amanda. "18 Essential Online Teaching Tools for Educators and Students." *Creately Blog*, 31 May 2021, www.creately.com/blog/education/online-teaching-tools/.

5. Athuraliya, Amanda. "The Essential Guide to Online Lesson Planning: Tips, Tools and Templates." Creately Blog, 21 Jan. 2021,

www.reately.com/blog/education/online-lesson-planning/.

6. Blackburn, Steven. "Teacher Mental Health Can Be Impacted by Online Learning." District Administration, 3 June 2020, www.districtadministration.com/online-learning-teacher-compassion-fatigue-teacher-mental-health/.

7. By, Written, et al. "Why Digital Equity Goes Beyond Just Giving Devices to Students." GoGuardian, www.goguardian.com/blog/technology/digital-equity-beyond-giving-devices-to-students/.

8. Center, Ky Counseling. "Mental Health Effects of Online Learning." Kentucky Counseling Center, 20 Apr. 2021, www.kentuckycounselingcenter.com/mental-health-effects-of-online-learning/.

9. Chauhan, Ashutosh. "11 Digital Education Tools For Teachers And Students." ELearning Industry, 12 May 2021, www.elearningindustry.com/digital-education-tools-teachers-students.

10. Chawla, Kunal. "4 Essential Tips for Teaching an Effective Online Course - EdSurge News." EdSurge, EdSurge, 27

Dec. 2018, www.ed-surge.com/news/2015-06-16-4-essential-tips-for-teaching-an-effective-online-course.

11. Chawla, Kunal. "6 Essential Tips for Planning an Effective Online Course - EdSurge News." EdSurge, EdSurge, 27 Dec. 2018, www.ed-surge.com/news/2015-06-11-6-essential-tips-for-planning-an-effective-online-course.

12. Ferlazzo, Larry. "Strategies for Teaching Online in the Age of the Coronavirus (Opinion)." Education Week, Education Week, 5 Mar. 2021, www.ed-week.org/teaching-learning/opinion-strategies-for-teaching-online-in-the-age-of-the-coronavirus/2020/03.

13. Game, Prodigy. "20 Classroom Management Strategies and Techniques [+ Downloadable List]." Prodigy Education, www.prodigygame.com/main-en/blog/classroom-management-strategies/.

14. Gewirtz, David. "Best Online Teaching Tools in 2021: Gear for Teachers." ZDNet, ZDNet, 3 Aug. 2020,

www.zdnet.com/article/best-online-teaching-tools/.

15. ISTE, Team. "5 Things Every Educator Should Know about Digital Equity." ISTE, 12 Apr. 2017, www.iste.org/explore/Lead-the-way/5-things-every-educator-should-know-about-digital-equity.

16. Keith R. Krueger, Marie Bjerede09/10/15. "How Digital Equity Can Help Close the Homework Gap." THE Journal, www.thejournal.com/articles/2015/09/10/how-digital-equity-can-help-close-the-homework-gap.aspx.

17. Minero, E. (2020, August 21). 8 Strategies to Improve Participation in Your Virtual Classroom. Edutopia. https://www.edutopia.org/article/8-strategies-improve-participation-your-virtual-classroom.

18. Nidhi Hebbar 7 months ago, et al. "Digital Equity in Education Is About More Than the Internet." - Technology, People and Policy, 12 Nov. 2020, www.protegopress.com/digital-

equity-in-education-is-about-more-than-the-internet/.

19. Pearson. (2020, March 24). 9 strategies for effective online teaching. The world's learning company. https://www.pearson.com/ped-blogs/blogs/2020/03/9-strategies-for-effective-online-teaching.html.

20. TeachThought Staff "30 Of The Best Tools For Remote Teaching And Learning |." TeachThought, 16 May 2021, www.teachthought.com/technology/best-remote-teaching-tools/.

21. Team, GoGuardian. "How to Write a Digital Lesson Plan: A Guide for Educators Teaching Online." GoGuardian, www.goguardian.com/blog/learning/how-to-write-a-digital-lesson-plan/.

22. YouTube. (2020). 7 Best Websites and Apps for Distance Learning. YouTube. https://www.youtube.com/watch?v=svmGQhQLuBQ.

23. YouTube. (2020). How To Teach Online (Top Tips for New Online Teachers!). YouTube. https://www.youtube.com/watch?v=x2AlLG1iBBE.

24. Paccone, Peter. "Building Rapport In the Online Environment - Peter Paccone." Medium, 11 Dec. 2020, ppaccone.medium.com/building-rapport-in-the-era-of-online-teaching.

25. "Strategies For Teachers Tackling Digital Equity In The Classroom." *Givingcompass*, 2019, givingcompass.org/article/strategies-for-teachers-tackling-digital-equity-in-the-classroom/?

26. "Why Teach Online?" *Why Teach Online?*, 2021, www.utep.edu/extendeduniversity/online-faculty-resources/why-teach-online.html.

ABOUT THE AUTHOR

Randy Bentinck is a dedicated, resourceful, and goal-oriented professional educator with a strong commitment to each student's social and intellectual development.

He is a graduate of the University of Guyana with a B.A. Degree in Fine Arts (Hons) and a Post-Grad Diploma in Education (Administration).

His twenty-five plus years of experience in teaching both in the traditional and online classroom locally and internationally has provided him with a wealth of experiences that allow him to speak on teaching online from the first-person perspective.

His superior interpersonal and communication skills to foster meaningful relationships
with students, staff and parents set him apart
from most of his peers.